THE LANGUAGE GYM

CATALAN SENTENCE BUILDERS

A lexicogrammar approach
Beginner to Pre-Intermediate

FIRST EDITION

Imprint: Independently Published

About the authors

Gianfranco Conti taught for 25 years at schools in Italy, the UK and in Kuala Lumpur, Malaysia. He has also been a university lecturer, holds a Master's degree in Applied Linguistics and a PhD in metacognitive strategies as applied to second language writing. He is now an author, a popular independent educational consultant and professional development provider. He has written around 2,000 resources for the TES website, which have awarded him the Best Resources Contributor in 2015. He has co-authored the best-selling and influential book for world languages teachers, "The Language Teacher Toolkit" and "Breaking the sound barrier: Teaching learners how to listen", in which he puts forth his Listening As Modelling methodology. Gianfranco writes an influential blog on second language acquisition called The Language Gym, co-founded the interactive website language-gym.com and the Facebook professional group Global Innovative Language Teachers (GILT). Last but not least, Gianfranco has created the instructional approach known as E.P.I. (Extensive Processing Instruction).

Dylan Viñales has taught for 15 years, in schools in Bath, Beijing and Kuala Lumpur in state, independent and international settings. He lives in Kuala Lumpur. He is fluent in five languages, and gets by in several more. Dylan is, besides a teacher, a professional development provider, specialising in E.P.I., metacognition, teaching languages through music (especially ukulele) and cognitive science. In the last five years, together with Dr Conti, he has driven the implementation of E.P.I. in one of the top international schools in the world: Garden International School. This has allowed him to test, on a daily basis, the sequences and activities included in this book with excellent results (his students have won language competitions both locally and internationally). He has designed an original Spanish curriculum, bespoke instructional materials, based on Reading and Listening as Modelling (RAM and LAM), and also co-founded the fastest growing professional development group for modern languages teachers on Facebook, Global Innovative Languages Teachers, which includes over 12,000 teachers from all corners of the globe.

Jaume Llorens has been teaching for 10 years in a variety of contexts, including high schools, language schools and universities. He holds Masters degrees in Literature and in Teaching Catalan and Spanish as Second Languages, and a PhD in Literary Studies. Jaume is bilingual in Catalan and Spanish, and also speaks fluent English and Finnish. He currently resides in Helsinki, Finland, where he teaches Spanish. He has been a valued member of the Sentence Builder book editiorial team since the beginning of the project, always adding value with his eagle-like attention to fine detail (often on a practically molecular level), impressive subject knowledge, both in Spanish/Catalan & also English, and wolf-like determination to get jobs done efficiently and to a very high level of quality.

Ester Borin Bonillo is a native of Girona and has taught for 23 years, including high schools and universities. She is currently working at Cardiff University teaching Spanish, and currently resides in Penarth. She holds a Masters degree in teaching Catalan and Spanish as foreign Language. She is fluent in three languages, and she is also learning others. Ester is a passionate user of the E.P.I. approach and has been teaching using this approach consistently for the past 5 years, and has enjoyed watching her students getting great results and growing in confidence while doing so. She also been a valued supporter, and also member of the Sentence Builder book team, and has been involved in several Sentence Builder book projects, in various editorial capacities. Her academic interests are in the study of language acquisition, comprehensible input and its impact on learner confidence and fluency.

Dedication

For Catrina
-Gianfranco

For Ariella & Leonard
-Dylan

For Adrian
-Jaume

For Rosa, Josep & Joan
-Ester

Acknowledgements

Writing a book is a time-consuming yet rewarding endeavour. Jaume would like to thank his parents, Jaci and Jacques, for their support along the years, and also Elina for her support during the work on this project.

Ester would like to give a huge thank you to special friends (Jesús, Valle, John, Ana, Beatriz and Pato) for your encouragement and support. I would like to thank to my family too, that despite you are far away I still have your warm support when is needed. And finally, I want to extend a mention to Jaume and Dylan for their tireless support and encouragement.

In addition, our heartfelt thanks to our team of guest proofreaders: Miquel Martí Danés, Roberto Jover Soro, Meritxell Castillejo Vallverdú, Amanda García Álvarez, Marta Bernad, Ana Falcó Sisternes, Anna Carrasco Salgueiro, Mar Maldonado and Joaquim de Prado. Their contributions have ensured not only a highly accurate book but also helped make several improvements in terms of choice of structures and lexis. Thank you for your lending your time and expertise to this project.

Our gratitude to Martin Lapworth for his time spent creating online versions of the Sentence Builders contained in this book. These are now available, via subscription, on SentenceBuilders.com. The feedback on the final draft, was instrumental in making some key content decisions and tweaks. Thank you.

Lastly, thanks to all the wonderful, supportive and passionate educators on Twitter who have helped enhance our book with their suggestions and comments, and to the members of the Global Innovative Language Teachers (GILT) Facebook group for their engagement with the Sentence Builders series. We consider ourselves very lucky to have such colleagues to inspire and spur us on.

Gràcies a tots.

Introduction

Hello and welcome to the first 'text' book designed to be an accompaniment to a Catalan, Extensive Processing Instruction course. The book has come about out of necessity, because such a resource did not previously exist.

How to use this book if you have bought into our E.P.I. approach

This book was originally designed as a resource to use in conjunction with our E.P.I. approach and teaching strategies. Our course favours flooding comprehensible input, organising content by communicative functions and related constructions, and a big focus on reading and listening as modelling. The aim of this book is to empower the beginner-to-pre-intermediate learner with linguistic tools - high-frequency structures and vocabulary - useful for real-life communication. Since, in a typical E.P.I. unit of work, aural and oral work play a huge role, this book should not be viewed as the ultimate E.P.I. coursebook, but rather as a **useful resource** to **complement** your Listening-As-Modelling and Speaking activities.

Sentence Builders – Online Versions

Please note that all these Catalan sentence builders are also available on the SentenceBuilders.com website, together with an extensive range of self-marking homework or class assignments, designed to practice listening, reading and writing in keeping with the EPI approach (available via subscription).

How to use this book if you don't know or have NOT bought into our approach

Alternatively, you may use this book to dip in and out of as a source of printable material for your lessons. Whilst our curriculum is driven by communicative functions rather than topics, we have deliberately embedded the target constructions in topics which are popular with teachers and commonly found in published coursebooks.

If you would like to learn about E.P.I. you could read one of the authors' blogs. The definitive guide is Dr Conti's "Patterns First – How I Teach Lexicogrammar" which can be found on his blog (www.gianfrancoconti.com). There are also blogs on Dylan's wordpress site (mrvinalesmfl.wordpress.com) such as "Using sentence builders to reduce (everyone's) workload and create more fluent linguists" which can be read to get teaching ideas and to learn how to structure a course, through all the stages of E.P.I.

The book "Breaking the Sound Barrier: Teaching Learners how to Listen" by Gianfranco Conti and Steve Smith, provides a detailed description of the approach and of the listening and speaking activities you can use in synergy with the present book.

The basic structure of the book

The book contains 19 macro-units which concern themselves with a specific communicative function, such as 'Describing people's appearance and personality', 'Comparing and contrasting people', 'Saying what you like and dislike' or 'Saying what you and others do in your free time'. You can find a note of each communicative function in the Table of Contents. Each unit includes:

- a sentence builder modelling the target constructions;
- a set of vocabulary building activities which reinforce the material in the sentence builder;
- a set of narrow reading texts exploited through a range of tasks focusing on both the meaning and structural levels of the text;
- a set of translation tasks aimed at consolidation through retrieval practice;
- a set of writing tasks targeting essential writing micro-skills such as spelling, functional and positional processing, editing and communication of meaning.

Each sentence builder at the beginning of a unit contains one or more constuctions which have been selected with real-life communication in mind. Each unit is built around that construction <u>but not solely on it</u>. Based on the principle that each E.P.I instructional sequence must move from modelling to production in a seamless and organic way, each unit expands on the material in each sentence builder by embedding it in texts and graded tasks which contain both familiar and unfamiliar (but comprehensible and learnable) vocabulary and structures. Through lots of careful recycling and thorough and extensive processing of the input, by the end of each unit the student has many opportunities to encounter and process the new vocabulary and patterns with material from the previous units.

Alongside the macro-units you will find:

- grammar units: one or two pages of activities occurring at regular intervals. They explicitly focus on key grammar structures which enhance the generative power of the constructions in the sentence builders. At this level they mainly concern themselves with full conjugations of key verbs, with agreement and preposition usage. Note that these units recycle the same verbs many times over by revisiting at regular intervals but in different linguistic contexts;
- question-skills units: one or two pages on understanding and creating questions. These micro-units too occur at regular intervals in the book, so as to recycle the same question patterns in different linguistic contexts;
- revision quickies: these are retrieval practice tasks aimed at keeping the previously learnt vocabulary alive. These too occur at regular intervals;
- self-tests: these occur at the end of the book. They are divided into two sections, one for less confident and one for more confident learners.

The point of all the above micro-units is to implement lots of systematic recycling and interleaving, two techniques that allow for stronger retention and transfer of learning.

Important *caveat*

1) This is a 'no frills' book. This means that there are a limited number of illustrations (only on unit title pages). This is because we want every single little thing in this book to be useful. Consequently, we have packed a substantive amount of content at the detriment of its outlook. In particular, we have given serious thought to both **recycling** and **interleaving**, in order to allow for key constructions, words and grammar items to be revisited regularly so as to enhance exponentially their retention.

2) **Listening** as modelling is an essential part of E.P.I. There will be an accompanying listening booklet released shortly which will contain narrow listening exercises for all 19 units, following the same content as this book.

3) **All content** in this booklet matches the content on the **Language Gym** website. For best results, we recommend a mixture of communicative, retrieval practice games, combined with Language Gym games and workouts, and then this booklet as the follow-up, either in class or for homework.

4) An **answer booklet** is also available, for those that would like it. We have produced it separately to stop this booklet from being excessively long.

5) This booklet is suitable for **beginner** to **pre-intermediate** learners. This equates to a **CEFR A1-A2** level, or a beginner **Y6-Y8** class. You do not need to start at the beginning, although you may want to dip in to certain units for revision/recycling. You do not need to follow the booklet in order, although many of you will, and if you do, you will benefit from the specific recycling/interleaving strategies. Either way, all topics are repeated frequently throughout the book.

We do hope that you and your students will find this book useful and enjoyable.

Gianfranco, Dylan, Jaume & Ester

TABLE OF CONTENTS

UNIT 1
Talking about my age

In this unit you will learn:

- How to say your name and age
- How to say someone else's name and age
- How to count from 1 to 16
- A range of common Catalan names
- The words for brother and sister

Tinc un any

Tinc deu anys

Tinc quinze anys

Tinc sis anys

UNIT 1
Talking about my age

				tinc *I have**	un	1	**any** *year*
Em dic *I am called*							
El meu germà *My brother* **La meva germana** *My sister* **El seu germà** *His/Her brother* **La seva germana** *His/Her sister*	**es diu** *is called*	Adrià Arnau Francesc Jan Miquel Pol Roger Alba Emma Júlia Laia Maria Martina Ona	**i** *and*	**té** *he/she has**	dos tres quatre cinc sis set vuit nou deu onze dotze tretze catorze quinze setze	2 3 4 5 6 7 8 9 10 11 12 13 14 15 16	**anys** *years*

__Author's note:__ In Catalan, we use the verb "to have" for age. So, we say "tinc deu anys" to say how old we are, even though it means, literally "I have ten years". There are a few romance languages (e.g. Spanish/Italian/French) that do this :D

Unit 1. Talking about my age: VOCABULARY BUILDING

1. Match

un any	seven years
dos anys	four years
tres anys	five years
quatre anys	six years
cinc anys	eleven years
sis anys	ten years
set anys	twelve years
vuit anys	nine years
nou anys	two years
deu anys	eight years
onze anys	one year
dotze anys	three years

2. Complete with the missing word

a. Tinc ______________ anys   *I am fourteen years old*

b. El meu germà ______ diu Pau   *My brother is called Pau*

c. Em ________ Dídac   *My name is Dídac*

d. El meu germà ______ dos anys   *My brother is two*

e. La meva germana té ________ anys   *My sister is four*

f. ______ dic Anna   *My name is Anna*

quatre	té	es
em	catorze	dic

3. Translate into English

a. Tinc tres anys

b. Tinc cinc anys

c. Tinc onze anys

d. Té quinze anys

e. Tenen tretze anys

f. Tenen set anys

g. El meu germà

h. La meva germana

i. Es diu

4. Broken words

a. Ti_____ *I have*

b. Em d____ *my name is*

c. La meva ger______ *my sister*

d. Qui_____ *fifteen*

e. Set______ *sixteen*

f. On_____ *eleven*

g. N_____ *nine*

h. Cato______ *fourteen*

i. Do_____ *twelve*

5. Rank the people below from oldest to youngest, as shown in the example

El Miquel té quinze anys	1
La Maria té tretze anys	
El Francesc té dos anys	
El Pau té quatre anys	
El Josep té un any	
La Daniela té cinc anys	
L'Arantxa té nou anys	
La Marta té tres anys	

6. For each pair of people write who is the oldest, as shown in the example

A	B	OLDER
Tinc onze anys	Tinc tretze anys	B
Tinc tres anys	Tinc sis anys	
Tinc onze anys	Tinc dotze anys	
Tinc quinze anys	Tinc tretze anys	
Tinc catorze anys	Tinc onze anys	
Tinc vuit anys	Tinc nou anys	
Tinc onze anys	Tinc set anys	

Unit 1. Talking about my age: READING

Em dic Nico. Soc argentí. Tinc dotze anys i visc a Buenos Aires, la capital d'Argentina. Tinc un germà que es diu Antonio. L'Antonio té catorze anys.
Nico, 12 anys. Buenos Aires

Em dic Rashid. Soc marroquí. Tinc deu anys i visc a Rabat, la capital del Marroc. Tinc una germana que es diu Naima i un germà que es diu Abdul. La Naima té cinc anys. L'Abdul té nou anys.
Rashid, 10 anys. Marroc

Em dic Marco. Soc italià. Tinc tretze anys i visc a Roma, la capital d'Itàlia. Tinc un germà que es diu Víctor. El Víctor té quinze anys.
Marco, 13 anys. Roma

Em dic Marine. Soc francesa. Tinc deu anys i visc a París, la capital de França. Tinc una germana que es diu Fabienne. La Fabienne té onze anys. També tinc un germà que es diu Pierre. El Pierre té vuit anys.
Marine, 10 anys. París

Em dic Kaori. Soc japonesa. Tinc set anys i visc a Tòquio, la capital del Japó. Tinc una germana que es diu Yoko. La Yoko té tretze anys. També tinc un germà que es diu Hiroto. El Hiroto té deu anys.
Kaori, 7 anys. Tòquio

Em dic Hans. Soc alemany. Tinc catorze anys i visc a Berlín, a Alemanya. Tinc dos germans. El meu germà gran es diu Patrick i el meu germà petit es diu Philip. El Patrick té setze anys i el Philip té quinze anys.
Hans, 14 anys. Berlín

1. Find the Catalan for the following items in Nico's text

a. I am Argentinian

b. I am called

c. the capital

d. in Buenos Aires

e. who is called Antonio

f. I am twelve

g. is fourteen

2. Answer the following questions about Rashid

a. Where is Rashid from?

b. How old is he?

c. How many siblings does he have?

d. What are their names and ages?

3. Complete the table below

	Age	Nationality	How many siblings	Ages of siblings
Marco				
Nico				
Rashid				

4. Hans, Kaori or Marine?

a. Who is from Germany?

b. Who has an 11-year-old sister?

c. Who is 7?

d. Who has an older brother aged 16?

e. Who has a 15-year old brother?

Unit 1. Talking about my age: TRANSLATION

**1. Faulty translation: spot and correct
(in the English) the translation mistakes**

a. Em dic Alba. *Her name is Alba.*

b. Tinc dues germanes. *I have two brothers.*

c. La meva germana es diu Marta.

   My mother is called Marta.

d. El meu germà té cinc anys. *My sister is 5.*

e. Tinc quinze anys. *I am five.*

f. El meu germà té vuit anys.

   My brother is seven.

g. No tinc germans. *I don't have a sister.*

h. Tinc setze anys. *I am 17.*

i. Tinc dotze anys. *I am 13.*

j. Es diu Joan. *My name is Joan.*

2. Translate into English

a. El meu germà es diu Joan.

b. Tinc quinze anys.

c. El meu germà té sis anys.

d. La meva germana es diu Emma.

e. Tinc set anys.

f. Visc a Barcelona.

g. La meva germana té catorze anys.

h. Tinc un germà i una germana.

i. La Maria té dotze anys.

j. L'Arantxa té nou anys.

3. Translate into Catalan

a. My name is Francesc. I am six.

b. My brother is fifteen years old.

c. I am twelve.

d. My sister is called Arantxa.

e. I am fourteen.

f. I have a brother and a sister.

g. My name is Pere and I am fourteen.

h. My name is Gabriel and I am eleven.

i. My name is Santiago. I am ten. I have a brother and a sister.

j. My sister is called Anna. She is twelve.

Unit 1. Talking about my age: WRITING

1. Complete the words

a. E___ d______ Francesc.

b. Ti______ cato________ a________ .

c. ______nc un__ g_____________a.

d. El m____ g___________à es d______ Julio.

e. Em ______c Albert.

f. El meu ______rmà e__ d___ Pau.

g. ______nc tr______e anys.

h. La meva g_________a es d______ Lola.

2. Write out the numbers in Catalan

a. nine   n_________________

b. seven   s_________________

c. twelve   d_________________

d. five   c_________________

e. fourteen   c_________________

f. sixteen   s_________________

g. thirteen   t_________________

h. four   q_________________

3. Spot and correct the spelling mistakes

a. Em tic Paco.

b. Tinc tretze añs.

c. El meu germà té cinco anys.

d. El meu hermà es diu Albert.

e. Im dic Ramón.

f. La meva germana es dic Alexandra.

4. Complete with a suitable word

a. La meva germana es

_________ Laura.

b. ____ _______ germà té

quinze anys.

c. Em _________ Marc.

d. Tinc un ___________ que

es diu Carles.

e. Tinc una ____________ que

es diu Arantxa.

f. El meu germà _____ catorze

anys.

5. Guided writing: write 4 short paragraphs in the first person singular (I) describing the people below

	Age	Lives in	Nationality	Brother's name and age	Sister's name and age
Samuel	12	Buenos Aires	Argentinian	Gonzalo 9	Eugenia 8
Rebeca	15	Madrid	Spanish	Jaime 13	Sofía 5
Michael	11	Berlin	German	Thomas 7	Gerda 12
Kyoko	10	Osaka	Japanese	Takumi 6	Rena 1

6. Describe this person in the third person (he)

Name: Jordi

Age: 12

Lives in: Barcelona

Brother: Oriol, 13 years old

Sister: Blanca, 15 years old

UNIT 2
Saying when my birthday is

In this unit you will learn to say:

- Where you and another person (e.g. a friend) are from
- When your birthday is
- Numbers from 15 to 31
- Months
- I am / He is / She is
- Names of Catalan speaking locations
- Where you live

UNIT 2
Saying when my birthday is

Em dic Josep *My name is Josep*	**soc de València** *I am from València* ***tinc 12 anys** *I am 12 years old*	**i** *and* **el meu aniversari és el** *my birthday is the*	1 - **un / u** 2 - **dos** 3 - **tres** 4 - **quatre** 5 - **cinc** 6 - **sis** 7 - **set** 8 - **vuit** 9 - **nou** 10 - **deu** 11 - **onze** 12 - **dotze** 13 - **tretze** 14 - **catorze** 15 - **quinze** 16 - **setze**		**gener** *January* **febrer** **març** **abril** **maig** **juny**
El meu amic es diu Gerard *My friend is called Gerard* **La meva amiga es diu Catalina** *My friend is called Catalina*	**és de Martorell** *he/she is from Martorell* **té 10 anys** *he/she is 10 years old*	**i** *and* **el seu aniversari és el** *his/her birthday is the*	17 - **disset** 18 - **divuit** 19 - **dinou** 20 - **vint** 21 - **vint-i-un/u** 22 - **vint-i-dos** 23 - **vint-i-tres** 24 - **vint-i-quatre** 25 - **vint-i-cinc** 26 - **vint-i-sis** 27 - **vint-i-set** 28 - **vint-i-vuit** 29 - **vint-i-nou** 30 - **trenta** 31 - **trenta-un/u**	**de/ d'** *of*	**juliol** **agost** **setembre** **octubre** **novembre** **desembre**

Author's note: *Don't forget!* Tinc/té *actually means "I have" and "he/she has" in Catalan. You use this verb for telling age. You will see it many times throughout this booklet!* ☺

Unit 2. Saying when my birthday is: VOCABULARY BUILDING

1. Complete with the missing word

a. Em _______________ Gonzalo   *My name is Gonzalo*

b. La meva __________ es diu Maria   *My friend is called Maria*

c. ___ _______ amic es diu Joan   *My friend is called Joan*

d. El meu ___________ és el…   *My birthday is on the…*

e. El _______________ de maig   *The fifth of May*

f. El _________________ de novembre   *The 18th of November*

g. El catorze de ______________   *The 14th of July*

h. ___ ______ aniversari és el…   *His/her birthday is on the…*

2. Match

abril	May
novembre	birthday
desembre	my friend (f)
maig	April
gener	November
febrer	he/she is called
aniversari	December
el meu amic	I am called
la meva amiga	February
em dic	January
es diu	my friend (m)

3. Translate into English

a. El catorze de gener

b. El vuit de maig

c. El set de febrer

d. El vint d'octubre

e. El dinou d'agost

f. El vint-i-cinc de juliol

g. El vint-i-quatre de setembre

h. El quinze d'abril

4. Add the missing letter

a. ani__ersari   c. ma__ç   e. a__ril   g. __ener   i. julio__   k. d__sembre

b. fe__rer   d. ma__g   f. jun__   h. a__ost   j. novem__re   l. set__mbre

5. Broken words

a. E___ t_______ d__ g__________   *3rd Jan*

b. E___ c_________ d__ j_________   *5th July*

c. E___ n_________ d'a___________   *9th Aug*

d. E___ d_______ d__ m__________   *12th March*

e. E___ s____________ d'a_______   *16th April*

f. E___ d__________ d__ d____________   *19th Dec*

g. E___ v_________ d'o______________   *20th Oct*

h. E___ v_____________ d__ m________   *24th May*

i. E___ t________ d__ s____________   *30th Sept*

6. Complete with a suitable word

a. Em _____________ Dylan

b. El meu ___________ és el dos de maig

c. Tinc nou _________

d. El meu ___________ es diu Gian

e. El Gian ___________ deu anys

f. El ______ aniversari és el tres de juny

g. La ___________ amiga es diu Verónica

h. El meu amic ____ diu Ronan

i. ___ ____ aniversari és el quatre d'agost

j. El vuit d'o_____________

Unit 2. Saying when my birthday is: READING

Em dic Roc. Tinc dotze anys i visc a Sabadell. El meu aniversari és el dotze de setembre. La meva amiga es diu Gabriela i té catorze anys. El seu aniversari és el vint-i-vuit de maig. En el meu temps lliure sempre toco la guitarra. La Gabriela també!
La meva amiga es diu Carlota. Té trenta-cinc anys i és professora. El seu aniversari és el vint-i-u de juny. La Carlota té un germà gran. El seu aniversari és el vuit de gener.
Roc, 12 anys. Sabadell

Em dic Sergio. Tinc vint-i-dos anys i visc a Oviedo, al nord d'Espanya. El meu aniversari és el deu de setembre. La meva amiga es diu Ivana i té quinze anys. El seu aniversari és el vint-i-vuit de maig. En el meu temps lliure sempre miro la tele.
Sergio, 22 anys. Oviedo

Em dic Lola. Tinc set anys i visc a Santiago, la capital de Xile. El meu aniversari és el cinc de desembre. Tinc dos germans, el Julio i l'Enrique. El Julio té onze anys i és molt simpàtic. El seu aniversari és el trenta de setembre. L'Enrique té tretze anys i el seu aniversari és el cinc de gener.
Lola, 7 anys. Santiago

Em dic Vicenç. Tinc vuit anys i visc a Perpinyà, al sud de França. El meu aniversari és el nou d'agost. La meva germana petita té quatre anys. És molt simpàtica. El seu aniversari és el nou d'agost. El mateix dia que jo!
El meu amic es diu Pau i té disset anys. El seu aniversari és el vint-i-cinc d'octubre.
Vicenç, 8 anys. Perpinyà

1. Find the Catalan for the following items in Roc's text

a. I am called

b. I am 12 years old

c. I live in Sabadell

d. My birthday is

e. the twelfth of

f. her birthday is on

g. in my free time

h. my friend

i. is called

j. she is 35

k. the 21st of June

l. has an older brother

m. the eighth of January

3. Answer the following questions about Lola

a. How old is she?

b. Where is Santiago?

c. When is her birthday?

d. How many brothers does she have?

e. Which brother is very nice?

f. How old in Enrique?

g. When is his birthday?

2. Complete with the missing words

Em dic Ana. _________ tretze

_______ i ________ a Madrid, __

Espanya. ____________ un gat a

casa. El meu _________________

és el vint–i–nou _____

desembre. El meu germà _____

nou _______ i el seu aniversari

és ___ l'abril.

4. Find someone who

a. ...has a birthday in December

b. ...is 22 years old

c. ...shares a birthday with a sibling

d. ...likes to play the guitar with their friend

e. ...has a friend who is 35 years old

f. ...has a birthday in late September

g. ...has a little sister

h. ...has a very nice sibling

i. ...is from the South of France

Unit 2. Saying when my birthday is: WRITING

1. Complete with the missing letters

a. Em d_ _ Fran

b. So_ d_ Barcelona

c. El m_ _ aniversa_ _ és el quin_ _ de jun_

d. Tin_ cat_ _ ze a _ ys

e. La meva ami _ a es di_ Catalina

f. La Catalina é_ de Madrid

g. El meu am _ c Albert é_ d_ Puigcerdà

h. L'Albert t_ onz_ a_ _s

2. Spot and correct the spelling mistakes

a. El meu anyiversari és el quatre de ener

b. Mi dic Fran

c. Soc di Barcelona

d. La meu amiga es dic Catalina

e. La Catalina ti onze anys

f. Jo tinc catorse ans

g. El mi aniversari és el primer de març

h. Tenc quince anys

3. Answer the questions in Catalan

a. Com et dius?

b. Quants anys tens?

c. Quan és el teu aniversari?

d. Quants anys té el teu germà/la teva germana?

e. Quan és el seu aniversari?

4. Write out the dates below in words, as in the example

a. 15.05 *el quinze de maig*

b. 10.06

c. 20.03

d. 19.02

e. 25.12

f. 01.01

g. 22.11

h. 14.10

5. Guided writing: write 4 short paragraphs in the first person singular (I) describing the people below

Name	Town/City	Age	Birthday	Name of brother	Brother's birthday
Bea	Girona	11	25.12	Josep	19.02
Àlex	Lleida	14	21.07	Ferran	21.04
Andreu	Palma	12	03.01	Pere	20.06
Carles	València	16	02.11	Toni	12.10

6. Describe this person in the third person (he)

Name: Marc

Age: 12

Lives in: Lleida

Birthday: 21.06

Brother: Joaquim, 16 years old

Birthday: 01.12

Unit 2. Saying when my birthday is: TRANSLATION

1. Faulty translation: spot and correct (in the English) the translation mistakes

a. El meu aniversari és el vint-i-vuit d'abril:
His birthday is on the 27th April

b. Em dic Robert i soc d'Espanya:
Your name is Robert and you are from Spain

c. Tinc vint-i-tres anys: *I am 22 years old*

d. El meu amic es diu Jordi:
My friend I am called Jordi

e. Té vint-i-sis anys: *I am 26 years old*

f. El seu aniversari és el quatre d'abril:
My birthday is the 14th April

3. Phrase-level translation: English to Catalan

a. My name is

b. I am ten years old

c. My birthday is the…

d. …the seventh of May

e. My friend is called Anna

f. she is twelve years old

g. her birthday is the…

h. the 23rd of August

i. The 29th April

Author's note: go back to e. Did you make Anna a girl? "amiga" Well done if you did! ☺

2. Translate into English

a. El vuit d'octubre

b. El meu aniversari és el…

c. El meu amic es diu…

d. El seu aniversari és el…

e. L'onze de gener

f. El catorze de febrer

g. El vint-i-cinc de desembre

h. El vuit de juliol

i. L'u de juny

4. Sentence-level translation: Eng. to Cat.

a. My name is César. I am 30 years old. I live in Spain. My birthday is on the 11th March.

b. My brother is called Pere. He is 14 years old. His birthday is on the 18th August.

c. My friend is called Joan. He is 22 years old and his birthday is on the 14th January.

d. My friend is called Angela. She is 18 years old and her birthday is on the 25th July.

e. My friend is called Anthony. He is 20 years old. His birthday is on the 24th September.

UNIT 3
Describing hair and eyes

In this unit you will learn:

- To describe what a person's hair and eyes are like
- To describe details about their faces (e.g. beard and glasses)
- Colours
- I wear
- He/she wears

You will also revisit:
- Common Catalan names
- The verb "Tenir" in the first and third person singular
- Numbers from 1 to 16

UNIT 3
Describing hair and eyes

Em dic *I am called* **Es diu** *He/she is called*	Anna Antoni Carles Dídac Emilia Isabel Josep Maria Pere	**i** *and*	**tinc** *I have* **té** *he/she has*	**sis anys** *6 years* **set anys** *7 years* **vuit anys** *8 years* **nou anys** *9 years* **deu anys** *10 years* **onze anys** *11 years* **dotze anys** *12 years* **tretze anys** *13 years* **catorze anys** *14 years* **quinze anys** *15 years* **setze anys** *16 years*	
Tinc els cabells *I have ... hair* **Té els cabells** *He/she has ... hair*	**castany<u>s</u>** *brown* **negre<u>s</u>** *black* **pèl-rojos** *red* **rossos** *blond*	**i**	**arrissats** *curly* **curts** *short* **de punta** *spiky* **llargs** *long* **llisos** *straight* **ondulats** *wavy* **rapats** *very short / crew-cut*		
Tinc els ulls *I have ... eyes* **Té els ulls** *He/she has ... eyes*	**blau<u>s</u>** *blue* **marron<u>s</u>** *brown* **negre<u>s</u>** *black* **verd<u>s</u>** *green*	**i**	**(no) porto** *I don't wear* **(no) porta** *he/she doesn't wear*	**barba** *a beard* **bigoti** *a moustache* **ulleres** *glasses*	

Unit 3. Describing hair and eyes: VOCABULARY BUILDING

1. Complete with the missing word

a. Tinc els cabells c__________   *I have brown hair*

b. Tinc els cabells r__________   *I have blond hair*

c. Porto b__________   *I wear a beard*

d. Tinc els ulls b__________   *I have blue eyes*

e. No porto u__________   *I don't wear glasses*

f. Tinc els cabells c_______   *I have short hair*

g. Tinc els ulls n__________   *I have black/dark eyes*

h. Tinc els cabells p__________   *I have red hair*

2. Match

Els cabells llisos	Black eyes
Els cabells negres	Moustache
Les ulleres	Green eyes
Els cabells rossos	Black hair
Els ulls negres	Short hair
El bigoti	Long hair
Els ulls blaus	Straight hair
Els ulls verds	Blonde hair
Els cabells curts	Glasses
Els cabells llargs	Blue eyes

3. Translate into English

a. Els cabells arrissats

b. Els ulls blaus

c. Porto ulleres

d. Els cabells rossos

e. Els ulls verds

f. Pèl-roig

g. Els ulls negres

h. Els cabells negres

4. Add the missing letter

a. Lla__gs   c. __abells   e. Bla__   g. Arrissa__s   i. Negr__s   k. Ul__s

b. Ull__res   d. Bigo__i   f. V__rds   h. Ll__sos   j. C__rts   l. Por__o

5. Broken words

a. T____ e___ c________ a__________   *I have curly hair*

b. P__________ u__________   *I wear glasses*

c. __i__ __l__ c________s c________   *I have short hair*

d. N__ p________ b__________   *I don't have a moustache*

e. ______c ____s u______ marrons   *I have brown eyes*

f. P____t__ b__________   *I have a beard*

g. T________ v______ a______   *I am eight years old*

h. E__ d___ Maria   *My name is Maria*

i. T______ n_____ a______   *I am nine years old*

6. Complete with a suitable word

a. Tinc deu __________

b. __________ barba

c. Em __________ Antoni

d. Porto __________

e. Tinc els __________ curts

f. No __________ ulleres

g. Tinc ______ ulls marrons

h. Tinc ______ cabells negres

i. No __________ bigoti

j. __________ els cabells llargs

k. ______ dic Pere

l. Tinc __________ anys

Unit 3. Describing hair and eyes: READING

Em dic Marta. Tinc dotze anys i visc a Malabo, la capital de Guinea Equatorial. Tinc els cabells negres, llisos i curts, i els ulls blaus. Porto ulleres. El meu aniversari és el deu de setembre. La meva germana té els cabells ondulats i té deu anys. **Marta, 12 anys. Malabo**

Em dic Alba. Tinc quinze anys i visc a Barcelona, la capital de Catalunya. Tinc els cabells castanys, ondulats i llargs, i els ulls blaus. No porto ulleres. El meu aniversari és el quinze d'octubre. **Alba, 15. Barcelona**

Em dic Alejandro. Tinc nou anys i visc a Santiago, la capital de Xile. Tinc els cabells castanys, ondulats i curts, i els ulls marrons. No porto ulleres. El meu aniversari és el cinc de desembre. El meu germà es diu Travis. Té quinze anys, és pèl-roig i té els ulls negres. Porta ulleres. El seu aniversari és el tretze de novembre. És molt musculós.

Alejandro, 9 anys. Santiago

Em dic Alina. Tinc vuit anys i visc a Quito, la capital de l'Equador. Tinc els cabells castanys, llargs i arrissats, i els ulls verds. Porto ulleres. El meu aniversari és el nou de maig. A casa tinc tres animals: un cavall, un gos i un gat. El meu germà es diu Sergio. Té catorze anys. Té els cabells rossos, llargs i llisos, i els ulls verds, com jo. També porta ulleres, com el meu pare. El seu aniversari és el dos de juny. És molt intel·ligent.
Alina, 8 anys. Quito

Em dic Pablo. Tinc deu anys i visc a Madrid, la capital d'Espanya. Tinc els cabells rossos, llisos i curts, i els ulls verds. Porto ulleres. El meu aniversari és el vuit d'abril.
Pablo, 10 anys. Madrid

1. Find the Catalan for the following in Marta's text

a. I am called:

b. In:

c. I wear glasses:

d. My birthday is:

e. The tenth of:

f. I have:

g. Straight:

h. Black:

i. The eyes:

2. Answer the following questions about Alba

a. How old is she?

b. Where is Barcelona?

c. What colour is her hair?

d. Is her hair wavy, straight or curly?

e. What length is her hair?

f. What colour are her eyes?

g. When is her birthday?

3. Complete with the missing words

Em dic Pau. _________ deu anys i visc __ València, la _________ de la Comunitat Valenciana. Tinc els _________ rossos, llisos i curts, i els _________ verds. _________ ulleres. El meu aniversari _____ el vuit __'abril.

4. Answer the questions below about all five texts

a. Who has a brother called Sergio?

b. Who is eight years old?

c. Who celebrates their birthday on October 15th?

d. How many people wear glasses?

e. Who has red hair and black-coloured eyes?

f. Who has a very intelligent brother?

g. Whose birthday is in April?

h. Who has brown, wavy hair and brown eyes?

Unit 3. Describing hair and eyes: TRANSLATION

1. Faulty translation: spot and correct (in the English) the translation mistakes

a. Tinc els cabells rossos — *I have black eyes*

b. Té els ulls blaus — *He/she has brown eyes*

c. Porto barba — *He has a beard*

d. Es diu Pere — *I am called Pere*

e. Té els cabells curts — *I have long hair*

f. Tinc els ulls blaus — *I have green eyes*

g. Visc a Menorca — *I am from Menorca*

2. Translate into English

a. Tinc els cabells rossos

b. Tinc els ulls negres

c. Té els cabells llisos

d. Porta ulleres i barba

e. Porto bigoti

f. Porto ulleres de sol

g. No porto barba

h. Tinc els cabells arrissats

i. Tinc els cabells llargs

3. Phrase-level translation: English to Catalan

a. 'The' blond hair

b. I am called

c. I have

d. 'The' blue eyes

e. 'The' straight hair

f. He/she has

g. Ten years

h. I have black eyes

i. I have nine years

j. 'The' brown eyes

k. 'The' black hair

4. Sentence-level translation: English to Catalan

a. My name is Mark. I am ten years old. I have black and curly hair and blue eyes.

b. I am twelve years old. I have green eyes and blond and straight hair.

c. I am called Ana. I live in Madrid. I have long blond hair and brown eyes.

d. My name is Laura. I live in France. I have black hair, very short and wavy.

e. I am fifteen years old. I have black, curly long hair and green eyes.

f. I am thirteen years old. I have red, straight long hair and brown eyes.

Unit 3. Describing hair and eyes: WRITING

1. Split sentences

Tinc els cabells	ulls verds
Porto	barba
Tinc els	rossos
Tinc els	i arrissats
Tinc els cabells rossos	cabells negres
Em dic	anys
Tinc deu	Marta

2. Rewrite the sentences in the correct order

a. cabells els tinc arrissats

b. porto no barba

c. dic em Ricard

d. pèl-roig soc

e. es germà diu Pau el meu

3. Spot and correct the grammar and spelling mistakes

a. Tinc els ull negres

b. El meu germà es diuen Antoni

c. Té els cabell arrissats

d. Es dic Marta

e. Tinc catorze años

f. Tinc els llisos cabells

g. Tinc el ulls verds

h. Porto barbes

i. Porto ullera

j. No port bigoti

4. Anagrams

a. callseb   *cabells*

b. rbaba

c. llus

d. nyas

e. usbla

f. soross

g. gresne

h. atsarriss

5. Guided writing: write 3 short paragraphs in the first person singular (I) describing the people below

Name	Age	Hair	Eyes	Glasses	Beard	Moustache
Lluís	12	Brown Curly Long	Green	Wears	Does not have	Has
Anna	11	Blond Straight Short	Blue	Doesn't wear	Does not have	Does not have
Aleix	10	Red Wavy Long	Black	Wears	Has	Does not have

6. Describe this person in the third person (he)

Name: Jordi

Age: 15

Hair: Black, curly, very short

Eyes: Brown

Glasses: No

Beard: Yes

UNIT 4
Saying where I live and am from

In this unit you will learn to talk about:

- Where you live and are from
- If you live in an apartment or a house
- What your accommodation looks like
- Where it is located
- The names of regions and cities where Catalan is spoken
- The verb 'I am'

You will also revisit:
- Introducing yourself
- Telling age and birthday

Saying where I live and am from

Em dic David i *My name is David and*	**visc en** *I live in*	**una casa** *a house*	**bonica** *pretty* **gran** *big* **lletja** *ugly* **petita** *small*		**al centre** *in the centre* **als afores** *on the outskirts* **a la costa** *on the coast*
		un pis *a flat*	**en un edifici antic** *in an old building* **en un edifici modern** *in a modern building*		
	visc a *I live in* **soc de / d'** *I am from*	Andorra la Vella	a Andorra		
		Fraga	a l'Aragó		
		L'Alguer	a Sardenya, a Itàlia		
		Perpinyà	al Rosselló, a França		
		Barcelona	a Catalunya		
		Girona			
		Lleida			
		Tarragona			
		Alacant	a la Comunitat Valenciana		
		València			
		Maó	a Mallorca,	a les Illes Balears	
		Palma	a Menorca,		
		Eivissa	a Eivissa,		

Unit 4. Saying where I live and am from: VOCABULARY BUILDING

1. Complete with the missing word

a. Visc en _______ casa bonica — *I live in a pretty house*

b. M'agrada el meu ________ — *I like my flat*

c. Soc ___ Terrassa — *I am from Terrassa*

d. ________ en un pis petit — *I live in a small flat*

e. Un pis en un ________ antic — *A flat in an old building*

f. _____ de Santiago, la capital de Xile — *I'm from Santiago...*

g. Visc en una casa ________ — *I live in an ugly house*

h. Visc a les ____________ — *I live on the outskirts*

2. Match

al centre	big
bonica	small
gran	old
edifici	pretty
antic	the centre
els afores	the coast
la costa	I am from
Espanya	the outskirts
soc de	ugly
lletja	I live in
petita	Spain
visc a	building

3. Translate into English

a. Soc d'Escòcia

b. Visc en una casa

c. El meu pis és petit

d. Soc de Palma, a Mallorca

e. en un edifici modern

f. Soc de Cardiff, la capital de Gales

g. Visc a un pis a la costa de…

h. Soc de Tortosa, a Catalunya

4. Add the missing letter

a. Perpi_yà

b. Caste_ló

c. Bar_elona

d. Tarra_ona

e. Val_ncia

f. P_lma

g. Ei_issa

h. Llei_a

i. F_aga

j. And_rra

5. Broken words

a. S_____ d___ l'A________, a I_____ .
   I am from l'Alguer, in Italy

b. V___ e___ u____ c______ a________ . *I live in an old house*

c. S___ d___ B________, l__ c_________ d__ C________ .
   I am from Barcelona, the capital of Catalonia

d. V______ e__ u___ p______ a l__ c________ d__ Mallorca.
   I live in a flat on the coast of Mallorca

e. V______ e___ u___ c______ p________ però b________ .
   I live in a small but pretty house

f. S___ d__ V_________ i v______ e___ u__ e_________
   a_________ . *I'm from València and I live in an old building*

g. S____ d____ R_________ . *I am from Reus*

6. Complete with a suitable word

a. Soc _____ Girona.

b. Visc _____ un pis bonic.

c. En un ___________ antic.

d. Visc en una casa al ___________ .

e. Barcelona és la capital de
   _______________ .

f. Visc en una casa _____________ .

g. ________ d'Andorra.

h. Visc en un pis _______________ .

i. Soc de Palma, a _______________ .

j. Visc en una casa a la ___________ .

Unit 4. Geography test: Using your own knowledge (and some help from Google/your teacher) match the numbers to the places where Catalan is spoken

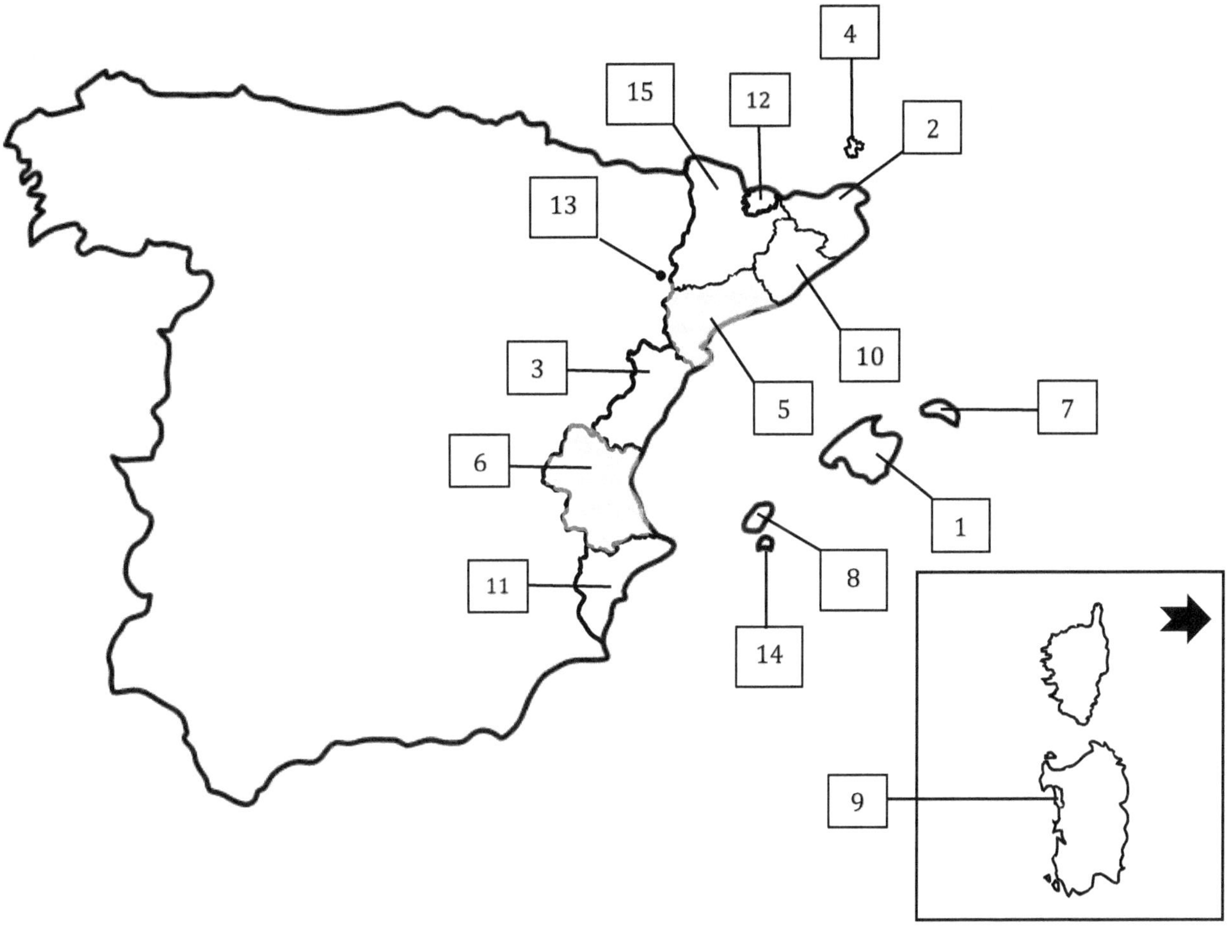

Catalunya	
Núm.	Ciutat
	Barcelona
	Tarragona
	Girona
	Lleida
Comunitat Valenciana	
Núm.	Ciutat
	València
	Castelló
	Alacant

Illes Balears	
Núm.	Ciutat
	Mallorca
	Menorca
	Eivissa
	Formentera
Altres llocs de parla catalana	
Núm.	Ciutat
	Andorra
	Perpinyà (Rosselló, França)
	Fraga (Franja de Ponent, Aragó)
	L'Alguer (Sardenya, Itàlia)

Unit 4. Saying where I live and am from: READING

Em dic Carles. Tinc vint-i-dos anys i el meu aniversari és el nou d'agost. Visc a Andorra la Vella, a Andorra. Visc en una casa bonica al centre de la ciutat. Tinc dos germans, l'Eduard i l'Enric. L'Eduard em cau molt bé, però l'Enric és molt estúpid. El meu amic Josep viu a Barcelona, a Catalunya. Ell viu en un pis en un edifici antic, també al centre.
Carles, 22 anys. Andorra la Vella

Em dic Isabel. Tinc vint–i–un anys i visc a Tarragona, a Catalunya, amb la meva amiga Marina. Vivim en un pis gran, bonic i modern als afores. El meu aniversari és el dos de juny i l'aniversari de la Marina és el dotze de juliol.

Al pis tinc un gos que es diu Miquel. És molt gran i bo. El seu aniversari és l'u d'abril. El Miquel té tres anys. També tinc una aranya, és bona però molt lletja, i es diu Lluïsa. L'aniversari de la meva aranya també és l'u d'abril. Llavors faig una festa per les dues mascotes a la vegada. És molt pràctic.
Isabel, 21 anys. Tarragona

Em dic Pau. Tinc quinze anys i visc a Barcelona, la capital de Catalunya. A la meva família som quatre persones: els meus pares, el meu germà Guillem i jo. El meu aniversari és l'onze de setembre i el del Guillem també, som bessons!
Pau, 15 anys. Barcelona

Em dic Estefania. Tinc nou anys i visc a València, a la costa d'Espanya. Visc en una casa amb la meva família: els meus pares, la meva germana gran, la Marta, i jo. El meu aniversari és el nou de maig i l'aniversari de la Marta és el trenta de març. Ella té onze anys. La meva casa és gran i bonica i està a la platja. M'agrada molt!
Estefania, 9 anys. València

1. Find the Catalan for the following in Isabel's text

a. My name is

b. I am 21 years old

c. I live in...

d. a big flat

e. on the outskirts

f. the 2nd of June

g. I have a dog

h. he is very big

i. his birthday is on the 1st April

j. is 3 years old

k. I also have a spider

2. Complete the statements below based on Carlos' text

a. I am _______ years old.

b. My birthday is the ____of ____________ .

c. I live in a ________ house.

d. My house is in the ________ of town.

e. I like Eduard but Enric is ____________ .

f. My friend Josep ________ in Barcelona.

g. He lives in an old _________ .

3. Answer the questions below about all four texts

a. How old is Pau?

b. Why do Pau and Guillem have the same birthday? *(what do you think a 'bessó' is?)*

c. Who only likes one of his siblings?

d. Who has two pets that share a birthday?

e. Why is it convenient that they share a birthday?

f. Who has a friend that lives in a different city?

g. Who lives with their really good friend?

h. Who lives in València?

i. Whose birthday is on the twelfth of July?

4. Correct any incorrect statements about Estefania's text

a. L'Estefania viu a Barcelona, la capital de Catalunya.

b. A la família de l'Estefania hi ha *(there are)* quatre persones.

c. El seu aniversari és al març.

d. L'aniversari de la Marta és el tres de març.

e. L'Estefania viu en una casa gran però lletja, a la platja.

f. A l'Estefania li agrada molt la seva casa.

Unit 4. Saying where I live and am from: TRANSLATION/WRITING

1. Translate into English

a. visc a

b. una casa

c. un pis

d. bonic

e. gran

f. en un edifici

g. antic

h. modern

i. al centre

j. als afores

k. a la costa

l. soc de

m. a Catalunya

n. a les Illes Balears

2. Complete with the missing words

a. Visc en una __________ lletja — *I live in an ugly house*

b. Un pis en un ___________ nou — *A flat in a new building*

c. Visc en un ______ petit — *I live in a small flat*

d. Una ________ a les _____________ — *A house on the outskirts*

e. _______ ___ Castelló — *I am from Castelló*

f. La _____________ de Catalunya — *The capital of Catalonia*

3. Complete the sentences with a suitable word

a. Visc a _______________ , a la Comunitat Valenciana.

b. Soc de Palma, a ________________________ .

c. Visc en un _________ bonic a les _____________ .

d. Visc en una casa bonica i _______________ .

e. _________ de Barcelona, la capital de _______________.

f. Visc en un ____________ modern al centre.

4. Phrase-level translation: English to Catalan

a. I live in…

b. I am from…

c. a house…

d. a flat…

e. ugly (m)…

f. small (m)…

g. in an old building…

h. in the centre…

i. on the outskirts…

j. on the coast…

5. Sentence-level translation: English to Catalan

a. I am from Maó, in Menorca, in the Balearic Islands. I live in a big and pretty house. I like my house.

b. I am from Barcelona, the capital of Catalonia. I live in a small and ugly flat in the centre.

c. I am from Andorra la Vella, in Andorra. I live in a flat in a new building on the outskirts. My flat is big but ugly.

d. I am from Castelló, in the Comunitat Valenciana. I live in a flat in an old building on the coast.

Unit 4. Saying where I live and am from: WRITING

1. Complete with the missing letters

a. Em d _ _ Fran

b. Vi_ _ en una ca_ _ bon_c_

c. V_s_ en un p_s gra_

d. _ _sc en una _ _sa al cent_ _

e. So_ d'Andorra

f. Jo _oc de Val_ncia

g. V_ _ _ en un pi_ pet_t a les afor_ _

h. _oc de Giro_ _ , a Catalu_ _a

2. Spot and correct the spelling mistakes

a. Soc de Valènsia, a Espania

b. Viv a Banyoles, a la província de Xirona

c. Visc en un casa lleig

d. Visc en un pis petita

e. Visc en un edifisi modern

f. Visc en Barcelona

g. Soy de Barcelona, en Cataluna

h. Soc en Mallorca, a les Isles Balears

3. Answer the questions in Catalan

a. Com et dius?

b. Quants anys tens?

c. Quan és el teu aniversari?

d. D'on ets?

e. On vius?

f. Vius en una casa o a un pis?

4. Anagrams: Catalan speaking regions and cities

a. dorAnra *Andorra*

b. lunyCataa

c. ncilèaVa

d. Iesll Barslea

e. L'guerAl

f. Pernyàpi

g. goTanarra

h. cantAla

i. naroGi

j. Eissavi

5. Guided writing: write 4 short paragraphs in the first person singular (I) describing the people below

Name	Age	Birthday	City	Country or region
Maria	12	20.06	Castelló	Comunitat Valenciana
Albert	14	14.10	Lleida	Catalunya
Andreu	11	16.01	Maó	Illes Balears
Carles	13	17.08	Andorra la Vella	Andorra
Laia	15	1.10	Vic	Catalunya

6. Describe this person in the third person (he)

Name: Jan

Age: 16

Birthday: 15 May

Place of origin: Perpinyà, France

Place of residence: Barcelona, Catalonia

UNIT 5
Talking about my family members, saying their age and how well I get along with them / Counting to 100

Revision quickie: Numbers 1-100 / Dates / Birthdays

In this unit you will learn to talk about:
- How many people there are in your family and who they are
- If you get along with them
- Words for family members
- What their age is
- Numbers from 31 to 100

You will also revisit
- Numbers from 1 to 30
- Hair and eyes description

UNIT 5
Talking about my family members, saying their age and how well I get along with them / Counting to 100

			un		any
A la meva família hi ha *In my family there is/are…*	**el meu avi, Jaume** *my grandfather*				
	el meu cosí, Miquel *my cousin*		dos		
			tres		
			quatre		
	el meu germà gran / petit, Dani *my big/little brother*	**Ell té** *He has*	cinc		
			sis		
			set		
			vuit		
Hi ha quatre persones a la meva família *There are <u>four</u> people in my family…*	**el meu pare, Joan** *my father*		nou		
			deu		
			onze	11	
			dotze	12	
			tretze	13	
	el meu tiet, Albert *my uncle*		catorze	14	
			quinze	15	
	la meva àvia, Neus *my grandmother*		setze	16	
			disset	17	anys
			divuit	18	
Em porto bé amb… *I get along well with…*			dinou	19	
	la meva cosina, Núria *my girl cousin*		vint	20	
			vint-i-un	21	
			vint-i-dos	22	
	la meva germana gran / petita, Clara *my big/little sister*	**Ella té** *She has*	trenta	30	
			trenta–un	31	
			trenta–dos	32	
			quaranta	40	
			cinquanta	50	
Em porto malament amb… *I get along badly with…*	**la meva mare, Blanca** *my mother*		seixanta	60	
			setanta	70	
			vuitanta	80	
	la meva tieta, Isabel *my aunt*		noranta	90	
			cent	100	

Unit 5. Talking about my family + Counting to 100: VOCABULARY BUILDING

1. Complete with the missing word

a. A la meva ____________ hi ha — *In my family I there is/are*

b. Hi ha ____________ persones — *There are five people*

c. El meu ____________ , Jaume — *My grandfather, Jaume*

d. El meu avi _________ vuitanta anys — *My grandfather is 80*

e. La meva ____________ Alba — *My mother Alba*

f. Ella _________ cinquanta anys — *She is 50 years old*

g. Em ________ bé amb el meu germà — *I get on well with my bro*

2. Match

Setze	12
Dotze	48
Vint–i–u	13
Deu	16
Trenta–tres	10
Tretze	21
Quaranta–vuit	15
Cinquanta–dos	5
Cinc	33
Quinze	52

3. Translate into English

a. Em porto malament amb...

b. La meva àvia

c. El meu tiet

d. Hi ha quatre persones

e. A la meva família

f. Em porto bé amb

g. El meu pare

h. Té vint anys

4. Add the missing letter

a. fam_lia

b. ti_c

c. p _rsones

d. a_i

e. ge _mà

f. gr_n

g. m_re

h. c_sí

i. em p_rto

j. b_

k. quin_e

l. de_

5. Broken words

a. H__ h__ s_______ p____________ a l__ m________

f____________ . *There are 6 people in my family.*

b. L__ m______ g____________ t__ d______ a_____ .

My sister is 12 years old.

c. A l__ m______ fam_______ hi ha... *In my family there is*

d. E__ m_____ c_________ e__ d_____ ...

My cousin (masc.) is called...

e. E__ m_____ p______ t__ c__________ –c_______

a______. *My father is 55 years old.*

f. E__ p_______ m_____________ a_____ e__ m_____

g________ g______ . *I get on badly with my older brother.*

6. Complete with a suitable word

a. A la ____________ família

b. ____________ tres persones

c. La meva germana ____________

d. Té catorze _______

e. La meva ____________ té trenta anys

f. Em porto _________ amb el meu pare

g. Hi ha quatre _________ a la meva família

h. Em ________ bé amb la meva àvia

i. No _____ porto bé amb el meu tiet

j. El meu cosí _____ quinze anys

k. Em porto bé _______ el meu avi

Unit 5. Talking about my family + Counting to 100: VOCABULARY DRILLS

1. Match

a la meva	there are
família	in my
hi ha	with
set	family
em porto bé	I get along well
amb	seven

2. Complete with the missing words

a. _____ _____ cinc persones — *There are five people*

b. El meu __________, Joan, té seixanta anys — *My father, Joan, is 60*

c. Em __________ bé amb el meu tiet — *I get along with my uncle*

d. Em porto ______________ amb el meu... — *I get along badly with my...*

e. La meva tieta _______ quaranta anys — *My aunt is 40*

f. Ell té ______________ anys — *He is 18*

g. Ella _______ vint-i-sis anys — *She is 26*

h. La meva __________ té vuitanta anys — *My gran is 80*

3. Translate into English

a. Ell té nou anys

b. Ella té quaranta anys

c. El meu pare té quaranta-quatre anys

d. Em porto malament amb el meu avi

e. Em porto bé amb el meu germà

f. La meva germana petita té cinc anys

g. Hi ha vuit persones a la meva família

h. A la meva família hi ha sis persones

4. Complete with the missing letters

a. El meu germà g _ _ n. *My older brother.*

b. A la meva fa _ _ lia h _ h_ tres persones.
In my family there are 3 people.

c. El meu cosí t _ di _ _u anys. *My cousin is 18.*

d. Em _ _rto molt m_ _ _ _ _ _ amb el meu germà. *I get along very badly with my brother.*

e. El meu ti_ _ té quaranta _n_s.
My uncle is 40 years old.

f. _ _ porto mo_ _ bé amb la meva cosina.
I get along very well with my cousin.

g. El meu c_ _í t_ q _ in_e anys.
My cousin is 15 years old.

h. Em porto així així _ _ _ ella.
I get along so so with her

i. Com e_ _ tu? *What are you like?*

5. Translate into Catalan

a. In my family

b. There are

c. My father

d. is 40 years old

e. I get along

f. with

6. Spot and correct the spelling mistakes

a. A la meva família hi hay tres personas

b. Mi àvia Angelina

c. El meu hermà te nou anys

d. Em porto mal amb meu cosí

e. El meu cosí té buit ans

f. El meu germà mayor

Unit 5. Talking about my family + Counting to 100: TRANSLATION

1. Match

Vint	30
Trenta	70
Quaranta	100
Cinquanta	50
Seixanta	20
Vuitanta	80
Noranta	40
Cent	60
Setanta	90

3. Write in the missing number

a. Tinc ____________–un anys   *I am 31*

b. El meu pare té ______________–set anys   *My dad is 57*

c. La meva mare té ______________–vuit anys   *My mum is 48*

d. El meu avi té ____________ anys   *My grandad is 100*

e. El meu tiet té ____________–dos anys   *My uncle is 62*

f. Tenen ________________ anys   *They are 90*

g. Els meus cosins tenen ____________–quatre anys   *My cousins are 44*

h. Té ______________ anys?   *Is he/she 70?*

2. Write out in Catalan

a. 35 *trenta-cinc*

b. 63 s____________________

c. 89 v____________________

d. 74 s____________________

e. 98 n____________________

f. 100 c____________________

g. 82 v____________________

h. 24 v____________________

i. 17 d____________________

4. Correct the translation mistakes

a. *My father is forty*   El meu pare té catorze anys

b. *My mother is fifty-two*   La meva mare té vint anys

c. *We are forty-two*   Tenim trenta-dos anys

d. *I am forty-one*   Quaranta-un anys

e. *They are thirty-four*   Tenen trenta-dos anys

5. Translate into Catalan. Please write out the numbers in letters

a. In my family there are 6 people.   ____.

b. My mother is called Marta and is 43.   ____.

c. My father is called Pere and is 48.   ____.

d. My older sister is called Laia and is 31.   ____.

e. My younger sister is called Marina and is 18.   ____.

f. I am called Daniela and am 27.   ____.

g. My grandfather is called Antoni and is 87.   ____.

Unit 5. Talking about my family + Counting to 100: WRITING

1. Spot and correct the spelling mistakes

a. cuaranta   *quaranta*

b. trenta i un

c. buitanta-dos

d. vintiun

e. nouranta

f. sent

g. setenta

h. setse

3. Rewrite the sentences in the correct order

a. la meva A quatre família persones hi ha
    In my family there are four people

b. bé amb porto el meu No germà em
    I don't get along with my brother

c. pare El meu es diu cinquanta-dos Miquel
    té i anys
    My father is called Miquel and is fifty-two

d. el meu pare i la meva jo A família la meva
    mare, hi ha persones: tres
    *In my family there are three people: my
    mother, my father and I*

e. es El meu cosí i anys Pep trenta-set diu té
    My cousin is called Pep and is thirty-seven

f. avi, i anys Ferran El meu vuitanta-set té es
    diu
    *My grandfather is called Ferran and is
    eighty-seven*

2. Complete with the missing letters

a. La meva ma_e t__ _uar_nta an_s.

b. El meu p_re té cin__uanta–un an__s.

c. Els meus av__s tenen vui__anta a__ys.

d. El me__ germ__ pet__t té v__nt an_ _ .

e. La m__va àv__a t_ no__anta a _ _ _ _ .

f. El meu g_ _m_ gra_ t_ tr_nta _ _ _ _ _ .

4. Complete

a. In my family: __ la m________ f___________

b. There are: H___ ___a

c. Who is called: Q______ e___ d_____

d. My mother: __a m________ m___________

e. My father: __l m________ p__________

f. He is fifty: T____ c____________ a_______

g. I am sixty: T_________ s__________ a______

h. He is forty: T____ q____________ a_______

5. Write a sentence for each person, as shown in the example

e.g. *El meu millor amic, que es diu Pep,*
     té quinze anys i em porto molt bé amb ell

Name	Relationship to me	Age	How I get along with them
e.g. Pep	*Best friend*	*15*	*Very well*
Roger	Father	57	Well
Cristina	Mother	45	Very badly
Sílvia	Aunt	60	Quite well
Dani	Uncle	67	Not well
Miquel	Grandfather	75	Very well

Revision Quickie 1:
Numbers 1-100, dates and birthdays, hair and eyes, family

1. Match

11	quinze
12	dotze
13	setze
14	divuit
15	onze
16	dinou
17	catorze
18	vint
19	disset
20	tretze

2. Translate the dates into English

a. El trenta de juny

b. El primer de maig

c. L'onze de setembre

d. El vint-i-dos de març

e. El trenta–u de desembre

f. El cinc de gener

g. El catorze d'abril

h. El vint-i-nou de febrer

3. Complete with the missing words

a. El meu aniversari _____ el setze d'abril.

b. Tinc catorze _________ .

c. El meu germà _____ els cabells ___________ .

d. ¿D' ______ ets?

e. A la meva família ___________ quatre persones.

f. La _________ mare té els ___________ marrons.

g. Soc ______ Irlanda.

h. El meu germà es _______ Robert.

on	és	d'	té	diu
rossos	ulls	anys	hi ha	meva

4. Write out the solution in words, as shown in the example

a. quaranta – trenta   *deu*

b. trenta – deu   _______________

c. quaranta + trenta   _______________

d. vint x dos   _______________

e. vuitanta – vint   _______________

f. noranta – cinquanta   _______________

g. trenta x tres   _______________

h. vint + cinquanta   _______________

i. vint + trenta   _______________

5. Complete the words

a. El meu a _ _   *My grandfather*

b. La meva co _ _ _ _   *My female cousin*

c. Els ul _ _   *The eyes*

d. Ve _ _ _   *Green (pl.)*

e. La ba _ _ _ _   *Beard*

f. Les ul _ _ _ _ _   *Glasses*

g. La meva ger_ _ _ _ _   *Sister*

h. T_ _ _ _   *I have*

6. Translate into English

a. La meva mare té els cabells castanys

b. Tinc els ulls blaus

c. Tinc quaranta anys

d. El meu avi té noranta anys

e. El meu pare porta ulleres

f. El meu germà porta bigoti

g. El meu germà té els cabells negres

h. La meva germana té els ulls grisos

UNIT 6: (Part 1/2)
Describing myself and another family member (physical and personality)

In this unit you will learn to say:

- What your immediate family members are like
- Useful adjectives to describe them
- The verb *ser* (to be) in the present indicative
- The verb *tenir* (to have) in the present indicative

You will also revisit

- Numbers from 1 to 31
- Hair and eyes description

UNIT 6 (Part 1/2)
Intro to describing myself and another family member

		MASCULINE	FEMININE
Jo	**soc**	**alt** *tall*	**alta** *tall*
		baix *short*	**baixa** *short*
		bo *good*	**bona** *good*
		fort *strong*	**forta** *strong*
		gras *fat*	**grassa** *fat*
		guapo *handsome*	**guapa** *pretty*
El meu germà gran *My older brother*		**lleig** *ugly*	**lletja** *ugly*
		musculós *muscular*	**musculosa** muscular
		prim *slim*	**prima** *slim*
La meva germana petita *My younger sister*	**és**	**avorrit** *boring*	**avorrida** *boring*
		antipàtic *mean*	**antipàtica** *mean*
		divertit *fun*	**divertida** *fun*
El meu pare *My father*		**dolent** *bad*	**dolenta** *bad*
		generós *generous*	**generosa** *generous*
La meva mare *My mother*		**simpàtic** *nice*	**simpàtica** *nice*
		tossut *stubborn*	**tossuda** *stubborn*

Unit 6. Vocabulary building

1. Match

Soc simpàtic	I am fun
Soc antipàtic	I am slim
Soc tossut	I am generous
Soc guapo	I am mean
Soc divertida	I am nice
Soc generós	I am short
Soc forta	I am strong
Soc dolent	I am good-looking
Soc baixa	I am bad
Soc alta	I am tall
Soc prim	I am stubborn

2. Complete

a. El meu germà petit és p________________ .
   My younger brother is slim.

b. El meu pare és s________________ .
   My father is friendly.

c. La meva germana gran és t________________ .
   My older sister is stubborn.

d. Soc m________________ . *I am muscular.*

e. El meu germà gran és d________________ .
   My older brother is fun.

f. El meu amic Pep és f__________ . *My friend Pep is strong.*

3. Categories: sort the adjectives below in the categories

fort   musculós   simpàtic   tossut
intel·ligent pacient   dolent   generós
gras   lleig   divertit   avorrit

El físic	La personalitat

4. Complete the words

a. Soc avor_ _ _ (m)

b. No soc lle_ _ (m)

c. Soc muscu_ _ _ _ (f)

d. Soc tos _ _ _ (m)

e. Soc dolen _ _ (f)

f. Soc gua _ _ (m)

g. Soc sim_ _ _ _ _ _ (f)

h. No estic gr_ _ (m)

5. Translate into English

a. La meva germana gran és generosa

b. El meu germà petit està gras

c. El meu germà gran és avorrit

d. La meva mare és divertida

e. No soc lleig

f. Soc una mica tossut

g. Soc molt guapo

h. El meu amic Valentí és fort

6. Correct the translation mistakes

a. Soc fort   *He is strong*

b. Està gras   *He is slim*

c. Soc molt guapa   *I am very ugly*

d. La meva mare és alta   *My mother is short*

e. La meva rata és lletja   *My rat is small*

f. La meva germana és tossuda *My sister is three*

g. El meu pare és dolent   *My father is good*

7. Complete

a. La me _ _   m _ _ _ _

b. La m _ _ _ _   g _ _ _ _ _ _ _

c. El me _   p _ _ _ _

d. S _ _ _   f _ _ _ _

e. Ell é _   to _ _ _ _ _

f. S _ _ _   si _ _ _ _ _ _ _

8. Translate into Catalan

a. I am strong and funny (f)

b. My mother is very stubborn

c. My sister is short and slim

d. My brother is intelligent

e. I am kind and fun (f)

f. My father is tall and fat

g. Gargamel is ugly and mean

h. I am tall and muscular (m)

Grammar Time 1: SER - To be (Part 1)

Feminine		
Jo	**soc** *I am*	alta antipàtica
Tu	**ets** *you are*	baixa grassa intel·ligent
Ella **La meva germana** **La meva mare**	**és** *she is*	pacient parladora *talkative* prima simpàtica
Nosaltres **La meva mare i jo**	**som** *we are*	altes antipàtiques
Vosaltres	**sou** *you are*	baixes grasses intel·ligents
Elles **les meves germanes**	**són** *they are*	pacients parladores primes simpàtiques
Masculine		
Jo	**soc** *I am*	alt antipàtic
Tu	**ets** *you are*	baix fort gras
Ell **El meu germà** **El meu pare**	**és** *he is*	intel·ligent pacient parlador prim simpàtic
Nosaltres **El meu pare i jo**	**som** *we are*	alts antipàtics
Vosaltres	**sou** *you are*	baixos forts
Ells **Els meus germans** **Els meus tiets**	**són** *they are*	grassos intel·ligents pacients parladors prims simpàtics

Present indicative of *ser* (to be) – Drills 1

1. Match

Som	I am
Són	You are
Soc	He is
Ets	They are
Sou	We are
És	You guys are

2. Complete with the missing forms of *ser*

a. (Jo) _________ molt parlador — *I am very talkative*

b. La meva mare _______ divertida — *My mother is funny*

c. Les meves germanes _________ parladores — *My sisters are talkative*

d. El meu gos ________ molt gandul — *My dog is very lazy*

e. Els meus pares ________ estrictes — *My parents are strict*

f. Com _______ ? — *What are you like?*

g. Com ________ els teus cabells? — *What is your hair like?*

h. Vosaltres _________ molt forts! — *You guys are very strong!*

3. Translate into English

a. El meu pare és simpàtic

b. La meva mare és parladora

c. Els meus germans són tímids

d. La meva germana petita no és molt alta

e. El meu millor amic és molt gras

f. El meu avi és molt amable

g. La meva germana gran és molt alta

h. Vosaltres sou molt forts!

4. Complete with the missing letters

a. Nosaltres s _ _ molt amables.
   We are very friendly.

b. La meva mare é _ molt estricta.
   My mother is very strict.

c. Els meus pares s _ _ molt pacients.
   My parents are very patient.

d. Els meus cosins s _ _ molt antipàtics.
   My cousins are very unfriendly.

e. El meu gat é _ molt gras. *My cat is very fat.*

f. Vosaltres s _ _ molt parladors!
   You guys are very talkative!

g. S _ _ una mica tímid. *I am a bit shy.*

h. Els meus avis s _ _ molt amables.
   My grandparents are very kind.

5. Translate into Catalan

a. You are: (tu) _ _ _

b. He is: (ell) _ _

c. You guys are: (vosaltres) _ _ _

d. They (f) are: (elles) _ _ _

e. We are: (nosaltres) _ _ _

f. She is: (ella) _ _

6. Spot and correct the grammar mistakes

a. La meva mare ets molt simpàtica

b. El meus pares és molt amables

c. La meva germana no és tossut

d. La meva germana i jo són alts

e. Com és tu?

Present indicative of *ser* (to be) – Drills 2

<table>
<tr><td>

7. Complete with the missing letters

a. So___ alts   *We are tall*

b. Et___ baix   *You are short*

c. El meu gos é___ gras   *My dog is fat*

d. Els meus professors s___n molt bons
  My teachers are very good

e. E___s molt guapa   *You are very pretty*

f. No s___c tímid   *I am not shy*

g. El meu germà i jo s___m molt treballadors
  My brother and I are very hard-working

</td><td>

8. Complete with the missing forms of the verb *ser*

a. La meva mare _______

b. Els meus pares ______

c. Jo _____

d. Elles _______

e. La meva mare i jo _______

f. El meu germà _______

g. Tu i les teves germanes _______

h. Tu _________

i. Vosaltres _________

</td></tr>
<tr><td>

9. Complete with the missing forms of *ser*

a. (Jo) _________ d'Andorra.

b. La meva mare __________ molt alta i guapa.

c. Els meus pares _________ molt estrictes.

d. El meu germà _________ molt amable.

e. (Jo) _________ guapo.

f. Elles _________ baixes.

g. El meu germà i jo _______ alts.

h. El meu cosí Marco _______ italià.

</td><td>

10. Translate into Catalan

a. My mother is tall

b. My father is short

c. My brother is not ugly

d. My sister is nice

e. My grandfather is strict

f. My grandmother is patient

g. My mother is intelligent

</td></tr>
</table>

11. Translate into Catalan. Remember that plural adjectives add an 's' (e.g. *alt – alts*). Make sure that the <u>words underlined</u> end in 's/es', as shown in the example

a. *My mother and my sister are very <u>tall</u>:* **La meva mare i la meva germana són molt alt<u>es</u>**

b. *My sisters are <u>**kind**</u> and <u>**nice**</u>:*

c. *My parents are very <u>**nice**</u>:*

d. *We (m) are <u>**talkative**</u> and <u>**lazy**</u>:*

e. *My brother and I are very <u>**tall**</u>:*

f. *My mother and my sister are <u>**beautiful**</u>:*

g. *My girlfriend and her sister are very <u>**short**</u>:*

Jo	**tinc** *I have*		
Tu	**tens** *you have*	**els cabells** *the hair*	**arrissats** *curly* **castanys** *brown* **curts** *short* **llargs** *long* **llisos** *straight* **negres** *black* **ondulats** *wavy* **pèl-rojos** *red* **rossos** *blond*
Ella **Ell** **La meva germana** **El meu germà** **La meva mare** **El meu pare**	**té** *he/she has*		
Nosaltres **El meu pare i jo** **La meva mare i jo**	**tenim** *we have*	**els ulls** *the eyes*	**blaus** *blue* **marrons** *brown* **negres** *black* **verds** *green*
Vosaltres	**teniu** *you guys have*		
Elles **Ells** **Els meus germans** **Els meus pares**	**tenen** *they have*		**grans** *big* **petits** *small*

Verb drills

1. Translate into English	**2. Spot and correct the grammar mistakes.** **Note: not all sentences are wrong**
a. Tenim els cabells negres	a. La meva mare té els cabells rossos
b. Té els cabells rossos	b. Les meves germanes teniu els cabells grisos
c. Tenen els cabells molt llargs	c. (Jo) té els cabells llargs
d. Tens els cabells molt curts	d. Ell tenen els cabells negres
e. Tenen els ulls verds	e. (Nosaltres) tenim els cabells curtes
f. Té els cabells pèl-rojos	f. Els meus pares té els cabells arrissats
g. Tenim els cabells arrissats	

3. Complete with the missing verb ending

a. (Jo) Ti____ els cabells rossos

b. La meva mare t____ els ulls blaus

c. Les meves germanes ten___ els cabells curts

d. El meu pare t___ els cabells grisos

e. (Nosaltres) te_______ els cabells negres

f. El meu avi t____ els cabells blancs

g. La meva mare i jo te____ els cabells blancs

h. El meu cosí t___ els cabells castanys

i. (Vosaltres) te_______ els cabells llargs?

j. El meu germà i jo ten_______ els cabells curts

k. El meu amic Pau t____ els ulls verds

l. Els meus germans te_______ els cabells curts

m. Jo ti___ els cabells llargs

n. (Tu) te___ els cabells llargs com la teva mare?

4. Complete with *té, tenim* or *tenen*

a. La meva mare _________ els cabells rossos

b. Els meus pares _________ els ulls marrons

c. La meva germana i jo _________ els cabells negres

d. Els meus avis _________ els cabells blancs

e. Els meus pares _________ els cabells negres

f. Les meves germanes _______ els cabells arrissats

g. La meva germana i jo _______ els cabells ondulats

h. El meu cosí _________ els cabells castanys

i. Les meves germanes _________ els cabells llisos

j. Nosaltres _________ els ulls blaus

5. Translate into Catalan

a. We have black hair

b. You have long hair

c. You guys have blue eyes

d. She has green eyes

e. My father has curly hair

f. My sister has straight hair

g. My uncle has grey hair

h. My grandfather has no hair

i. My father and I have blond hair

j. My uncle David has green eyes

6. Guided writing: write a text in the first person singular (I) including the details below

- Say you are 9 years old
- Say you have a brother and a sister
- Say your brother is 15
- Say he has brown, straight, short hair and green eyes
- Say he is tall and handsome
- Say she is 12
- Say she has black, curly, long hair and brown eyes
- Say your parents are tall, have black hair and brown eyes

7. Write short text in which you describe four relatives or friends. You must include their

a. name
b. age
c. hair (colour, length and type)
d. eye colour
e. if they wear glasses or not
f. their physical description
g. their personality description

UNIT 6 (Part 2/2)
Describing my family and saying why I like/dislike them

A la meva família hi ha *In my family there is…* **Hi ha quatre persones a la meva família** *There are <u>four</u> people in my family*	**el meu avi** *my grandfather* **el meu cosí** *my cousin* **el meu germà gran / petit** *my big/little brother* **el meu pare** *my father* **el meu tiet** *my uncle*	**El meu ____ m'agrada perquè és** *I like my ____ because he is* **El meu pare és bastant** *My dad is quite* **El meu pare és molt** *My dad is very* **El meu pare també és una mica** *My dad is also a bit*	**alt** *tall* **baix** *short* **bo** *good* **fort** *strong* **gras** *fat* **guapo** *handsome* **prim** *slim* **antipàtic** *mean* **divertit** *fun* **generós** *generous* **intel·ligent** *clever* **simpàtic** *nice* **tossut** *stubborn*
Em porto bé amb *I get along well with…* **Em porto malament amb** *I get along badly with…*	**la meva àvia** *my grandmother* **la meva cosina** *my cousin* **la meva germana gran / petita** *my big/little sister* **la meva mare** *my mother* **la meva tieta** *my aunt*	**La meva ____ m'agrada perquè és** *I like my ____ because she is* **La meva mare és bastant** *My mum is quite* **La meva mare és molt** *My mum is very* **La meva mare també és una mica** *My mum is also a bit*	**alta** *tall* **baixa** *short* **bona** *good* **forta** *strong* **grassa** *fat* **guapa** *pretty* **prima** *slim* **antipàtica** *mean* **divertida** *fun* **generosa** *generous* **intel·ligent** *clever* **simpàtica** *nice* **tossuda** *stubborn*

Unit 6. Describing my family: VOCABULARY BUILDING

1. Complete with the missing word

a. A la meva família h__ h__   *In my family there is*

b. Hi ha __________ persones   *There are 4 people*

c. La meva __________   *My mother*

d. Em porto __________ amb   *I get along well with*

e. Em porto __________ amb   *I get along badly with*

f. El meu ______ és molt alt   *My uncle is very tall*

g. La meva ______ és molt simpàtica   *My aunt is very nice*

h. La meva cosina és __________   *My cousin is fun*

2. Match

La meva tieta	My cousin (f)
El meu avi	My granddad
La meva mare	My mum
El meu pare	My dad
El meu germà gran	My aunt
El meu cosí	My little bro
El meu germà petit	My big bro
El meu tiet	My uncle
La meva germana	My sister
La meva cosina	My cousin (m)

3. Translate into English

a. El meu tiet m'agrada

b. La meva cosina és generosa

c. Té els cabells rossos

d. Em porto bé amb

e. No m'agrada el meu

f. Em porto malament amb

g. És tossut

h. És tranquil·la

4. Add the missing letter

a. Tos_ut   c. _impàtic   e. _osí   g. Gr_n   i. Tamb_   k. M'agra_a

b. Em p_rto   d. _vi   f. _etit   h. M_re   j. _iet   l. Per_uè

5. Broken words

a. A l__ m______ fam______ h___ h___

    In my family there is...

b. Q__________ p____________

    Four people

c. L__ m__________ m__________ é__ m _____ s____________

    My mother is very nice

d. E__ p__________ b__ a______ l__ m____________ ...

    I get on well with my (fem.) ...

e. E__ m______ t______ é__ m________ g________________

    My uncle is very generous

f. E __ p________ m ____________ a_____ e__ m______ ...

    I get on badly with my (masc.) ...

g. L__ m________ g__________ t__ e____ c__________ l_____

    My sister has long hair

h. E__ m______ p______ é__ b____________ i____________

    My father is quite clever

6. Complete with a suitable word

a. Tinc quatre ______________

b. __________ simpàtica

c. Em __________ bé

d. És molt ______________

e. Té els ______________ rossos

f. M'____________ la meva mare

g. Em porto ______ amb el meu tiet

h. Té els cabells negres i __________

i. Té els __________ blaus

j. El meu cosí és __________ divertit

k. La meva __________ és intel·ligent

l. La meva àvia té vuitanta __________

Unit 6. Describing my family: READING

Soc el Carles. Tinc deu anys i visc a Kuala Lumpur, la capital de Malàisia. A la meva família hi ha cinc persones: el meu pare, la meva mare i els meus dos germans, el Miquel i el Martí. Em porto molt bé amb el Miquel perquè és molt simpàtic i generós, però em porto malament amb el Martí perquè és molt dolent! **Carles, 10. KL**

Em dic Vero. Tinc catorze anys i visc a l'Aragó, a l'est Espanya. M'agrada molt el meu avi perquè és molt divertit. És intel·ligent però molt tímid.
El meu pare està molt gras i és molt tossut. Té els ulls marrons i porta els cabells rapats.
Vero, 14 anys. Aragó

Em dic Núria. Tinc quinze anys i visc a Girona, al nord-est de Catalunya. Tinc els cabells rossos i rapats. A la meva família hi ha sis persones. No em porto bé amb la meva germana perquè és estúpida i tossuda. Em porto molt bé amb els meus cosins perquè són molt simpàtics. El meu cosí preferit és diu Pau i és alt i fort. És molt divertit i simpàtic. Té els cabells negres i curts, i porta ulleres.
Núria, 15 anys. Girona

Em dic Pere. Tinc deu anys i visc a València, a la costa d'Espanya. Soc molt guapo. A la meva família hi ha moltes persones, vuit en total. El meu tiet m'agrada, però no m'agrada la meva tieta. Em porto molt bé amb el meu tiet Cèsar perquè és divertit i simpàtic, però la meva tieta Maria és antipàtica i horrible. Ella té els cabells rossos, llargs i arrissats, i els ulls blaus com jo. El seu aniversari és el deu de maig. **Pere, 10. Val.**

Em dic Guillem. Tinc nou anys i visc a Manresa, a Catalunya. A la meva família hi ha quatre persones. Em porto malament amb el meu pare perquè és molt tossut i antipàtic. La meva àvia m'agrada perquè és molt bona. **Guillem, 9 anys. Manresa**

1. Find the Catalan for the following items in Vero's text

a. I am called:

b. in the east:

c. my grandfather:

d. but:

e. very:

f. my father:

g. brown eyes:

h. shaved hair:

2. Answer the following questions about Pere

a. How old is he?

b. Where is he from?

c. How many people are there in his family?

d. Who does he get along well with?

e. Why does he like Cèsar?

f. Who does he not like?

g. When is her birthday?

3. Complete with the missing words

Em   dic   Clara. __________ deu anys i visc ___ Berga. A la meva família hi ha quatre __________.

Em _______ bé amb el meu avi perquè _____ molt simpàtic. El meu pare té els _________ curts i els _______ verds.

4. Find someone who

a. ...has a granny who is very good

b. ...is fifteen years old

c. ...celebrates their birthday on 10th May

d. ...has a favourite cousin

e. ...is from Aragó

f. ...only gets along well with one of his brothers

g. ...has a shaved head

h. ...thinks he is very handsome

i. ...is nine years old

Unit 6. Describing my family: TRANSLATION

1. Faulty translation: spot and correct (in the English) the translation mistakes

a. A la meva família hi ha quatre persones.

In my family there are fourteen people.

b. Mi madre i el meu germà.

My mother and my cousin.

c. Em porto malament amb el meu pare.

I get on well with my father.

d. El meu tiet es diu Iván. *My father is called Iván.*

e. Ell és molt simpàtic i divertit.

He is very mean and fun.

2. Translate into English

a. M'agrada el meu avi.

b. La meva àvia és molt bona.

c. El meu cosí té els cabells rapats.

d. El porto bé amb el meu germà gran.

e. Em porto malament amb la meva cosina.

f. El meu avi m'agrada perquè és molt generós.

g. El meu pare és simpàtic i divertit.

h. No m'agrada el meu germà petit.

i. Em porto malament amb el meu cosí Xavi.

3. Phrase-level translation: English to Catalan

a. He is nice

b. She is generous

c. I get along well with

d. I get along badly with

e. My uncle is fun

f. My little brother

g. I like my cousin Maria

h. She has short and black hair

i. He has blue eyes

j. I don't like my granddad

k. He is very stubborn

4. Sentence-level translation: Eng. to Cat.

a. My name is Oriol. I am nine years old. In my family there are four people.

b. My name is Carla. I have blue eyes. I get along well with my brother.

c. I get along badly with my brother because he is stubborn.

d. My name is Frank. I live in Mallorca. I like my uncle David because he is nice.

e. I like my cousin a lot because she is very good.

f. In my family there are five people. I like my father, but I do not like my mother.

Unit 6. Describing my family: WRITING

1. Split sentences

El meu pare és	cabells negres
La meva mare és	bé amb
Té els	el meu tiet
Té els	simpàtic
No m'agrada	ulls negres
M'agrada la meva	generosa
Em porto	tieta

2. Rewrite the sentences in the correct order

a. meva hi ha sis a la persones família

b. meu bé amb el em porto germà

c. tiet no el m'agrada meu

d. la meva blaus té els ulls mare

e. simpàtica molt la meva tieta és i divertida

f. ulls els negres tinc

3. Spot and correct the grammar and spelling mistakes

a. A la meu família hi ha

b. Em porta bé amb

c. No m'agrado la meva tieta

d. La meva germana és divertit

e. Em porto mal amb

f. El meu pare és generosa

g. Té els ull blau

h. La meva germana és guapo

i. Té el cabell rapats

j. Me agrada la meva àvia

4. Anagrams

a. fímalia

b. pirm

c. assarg

d. pagua

e. inl·ligtenet

f. mispàtica

g. tsosut

h. verditida

5. Guided writing: write 3 short paragraphs in the first person singular (I) describing the people below

Name	Age	Family	Likes	Likes	Dislikes
Albert	12	4 people	Mother because very nice. Has long blond hair.	Older brother because fun and very good.	Cousin Gemma because she is not nice.
Leo	11	5 people	Father because very fun. Has short black hair.	Grandmother because very nice and generous.	Uncle Edu because stubborn.
Manel	10	6 people	Grandfather because very funny. Has very short hair.	Younger sister because very good	Aunt Carolina because very strong but stubborn.

6. Describe this person in the 3rd person (he)

Name: Uncle Toni
Hair: Blond, shaved
Eyes: Blue
Opinion: Like a lot
Physical: Tall and strong
Personality: Nice, fun, generous.

UNIT 7
Talking about pets

Grammar Time: TENIR (pets and description)
Questions skills: Age / Descriptions / Pets

In this unit will learn how to say in Catalan
- What pets you have at home
- What pet you would like to have
- What their name is
- Some more adjectives to describe appearance and personality
- Key question words

You will also learn how to ask questions about
- Name / age / appearance / quantity

You will revisit the following
- Introducing oneself
- Family members
- Describing people
- The verb 'tenir' (to have) in the present indicative

UNIT 7
Talking about pets

	un mico *a monkey*	que es diu Alfons *that is called Alfons*
A casa tinc *At home I have* **No tinc** *I don't have*	**un ànec** *a duck* **un cavall** *a horse* **un conill** *a rabbit* **un conillet d'Índies** *a guinea pig* **un gat** *a cat* **un gos** *a dog* **un hàmster** *a hamster* **un lloro** *a parrot* **un ocell** *a bird* **un peix** *a fish* **un pingüí** *a penguin* **un ratolí** *a mouse*	**gran** *big* **petit** *small* **blanc** *white* **blau** *blue* **groc** *yellow* **negre** *black* **taronja** *orange* **verd** *green* **vermell / roig** *red* **afectuós** *affectionate* **animat** *lively* **avorrit** *boring* **bonic / preciós** *pretty* **divertit** *fun* **graciós** *funny* **lleig** *ugly*
	una gallina *a chicken*	que es diu Nayali *that is called Nayali*
El meu amic Borja té *My friend Borja has*	**una aranya** *a spider* **una rata** *a rat* **una serp** *a snake* **una tortuga** *a turtle* **una vaca** *a cow*	**gran** *big* **petita** *small* **blanca** *white* **blava** *blue* **groga** *yellow* **negra** *black* **taronja** *orange* **verda** *green* **vermella / roja** *red* **afectuosa** *affectionate* **animada** *lively* **avorrida** *boring* **bonica / preciosa** *pretty* **divertida** *fun* **graciosa** *funny* **lletja** *ugly*
M'agradaria tenir *I would like to have* **Li agradaria tenir** *He/She would like to have*		**un gat** *a cat* **una tortuga** *a turtle*

Unit 7. Talking about pets: VOCABULARY BUILDING

1. Complete with the missing word

a. A casa tinc un o___________   *At home I have a bird*

b. No tinc un c___________   *I don't have a rabbit*

c. M'agradaria tenir un g________   *I'd like to have a dog*

d. M'agradaria tenir una t__________   *I would like to have a turtle*

e. ___ casa tinc un g______   *At home I have a cat*

f. No tinc una s___________   *I don't have a snake*

g. T_______ una aranya a casa   *I have a spider at home*

h. M'____________ tenir un hàmster   *I'd like to have a hamster*

2. Match

un gat	a rat
un gos	a hamster
un cavall	two fish
un ocell	a cat
un peix	a turtle
una tortuga	a fish
un hàmster	a snake
un lloro	a dog
dos peixos	a parrot
una rata	a bird
una serp	a horse

3. Translate into English

a. Tinc un gos

b. La meva amiga té un ratolí

c. Tinc dos peixos

d. No tinc animals a casa

e. Tinc tres gossos

f. M'agradaria tenir una serp

g. El meu germà té una tortuga

h. El meu gat té cinc anys

4. Add the missing letter

a. El meu ami__   e. Un pe__x

b. Una tortu__a   f. Una __ata

c. Un l__oro   g. Un __nec

d. Dos pei__os   h. Un o__ell

5. Anagrams

a. sog *gos*   e. ollro

b. agt   f. reps

c. tugator   g. nyaraa

d. epix   h. cinoll

6. Broken words

a. A c________ t__________ u__ g____________.

   At home I have a dog.

b. E__ m______ a________ Pau t__ u__ l________.

   My friend Pau has a parrot.

c. E__ m_____ g_________ t___ u_____ t______________.

   My brother has a turtle.

d. N__ t______ u c___________. *I don't have a rabbit.*

e. T_______ u_____ s__________. *I have a snake.*

f. L'Àlex t_____ u__ g______. *Àlex has a cat.*

g. T_______ u__ p______ b_________. *I have a blue fish.*

h. T______ d______ a___________. *I have two animals.*

7. Complete with a suitable word

a. Tinc deu ________.

b. El meu peix es _________ Rex.

c. El meu _________ Pau té un lloro.

d. El meu germà ________ una rata.

e. ____ casa tinc dues mascotes.

f. ______casa tinc dues mascotes, un gos i una ____________.

g. A casa _______ un conill.

h. A casa tinc ______ ocell.

i. La meva germana _____ un cavall.

j. El meu _________ és blanc i marró.

Unit 7. Talking about pets: READING

Em dic Elena. Tinc vuit anys i visc a Barcelona. A la meva família hi ha quatre persones: els meus pares i el meu germà petit que es diu Marcel. El Marcel és molt antipàtic i pesat. Tenim dues mascotes: un gos que es diu Bo i un gat que es diu Dolent. El Bo és molt afectuós, i el Dolent és molt antipàtic, com el meu germà!
Elena, 8 anys. Barcelona

Em dic Robert. Tinc nou anys i visc a València. A la meva família hi ha quatre persones: els meus pares i el meu germà gran, que es diu Francesc. Ell té dotze anys i és molt divertit. Tenim dues mascotes: un lloro que es diu Ric i un gat que es diu Pobre. El Ric és molt parlador. El Pobre és molt juganer, igual que el meu germà! **Robert, 9 anys. València**

Em dic Juli. Tinc nou anys i visc a Llers. A la meva família hi ha els meus pares i els meus dos germans, que es diuen Jordi i Manel. El   Jordi és molt parlador i graciós. El Manel és molt seriós i treballador. Tenim dues mascotes a casa: un conillet d'Índies que es diu Sam i una tortuga que es diu Despacito. El conillet d'Índies és molt divertit i animat. El Despacito és molt seriós, igual que el meu germà Manel. **Juli, 9 anys. Llers**

Em dic Sònia. Tinc deu anys. A la meva família hi ha quatre persones: els meus pares i dues germanes petites, que es diuen Martina i Naia. La Martina és molt generosa, i la Naia és molt tossuda i avorrida. Tenim dues mascotes: un conill que es diu Busy i un ànec que es diu Loco. El Busy es molt tranquil i amable. El Loco és molt sorollós i animat, igual que la meva germana! **Sònia, 10 anys**

1. Find the Catalan for the following in Elena's text

a. two pets

b. which is called

c. a cat

d. a dog

e. very affectionate

f. like my brother

g. my parents

h. my name is

i. very unfriendly

j. four people

2. Find someone who

a. ...has a cat

b. ...has a parrot

c. ...has a duck

d. ...has a guinea pig

e. ...has a rabbit

f. ...has a dog

3. Answer the following questions about Juli

a. Where does Juli live?

b. What is his brother Manel like?

c. Who is fun and lively?

d. Who is like Manel?

e. Who is Jordi?

f. Who is Despacito?

g. Who is Sam?

5. Fill in the blanks

Em d_______ Fran. Tinc onze a_________ i v_________ a Banyoles. A casa m_______ hi ha cinc persones: els meus pares i les m_________ dues germanes, que es d___________ Aina i Marta. L'Aina ___s molt parladora i amable. La Marta és m______ mandrosa i antipàtica. T_________ dues mascotes a casa: una rata que ___s diu Maya i una gata que es diu Swift. És m_____ divertida i animada. La Maya é___ molt amable, c_________ la meva g____________ Marta.

4. Fill in the table below

Name	Elena	Robert
Age		
City		
Pets		
Description of pets		

Unit 7. Talking about pets: TRANSLATION

1. Faulty translation: spot and correct (in the English) the translation mistakes

a. A la meva família hi ha quatre persones i dues mascotes. *In my family there are four people and three pets.*

b. A casa tenim dues mascotes: un gos i una rata. *At home we have two pets: a dog and a rabbit.*

c. El meu amic té una tortuga que es diu Speedy. L'Speedy és molt graciosa. *My friend has a duck called Speedy. Speedy is very boring.*

d. El meu germà té un cavall que es diu Dylan. *My sister has a parrot called Dylan.*

e. La meva mare té un conillet d'Índies que es diu Nicole. *My father has a frog called Nicole.*

f. Tinc un gat que es diu Sleepy. L'Sleepy és molt animat. *I have a dog called Sleepy. Sleepy is very beautiful.*

2. Translate into English

a. Un gat divertit

b. Un gos afectuós

c. Un ànec graciós

d. Una tortuga avorrida

e. Un cavall preciós

f. Una rata animada

g. Un conillet d'Índies curiós

h. Tinc dues mascotes

i. A casa no tenim mascotes

j. M'agradaria tenir un gos

k. M'agradaria tenir un peix

l. Tinc un hàmster, però m'agradaria tenir una serp

3. Phrase-level translation: Eng. to Cat.

a. A boring dog

b. A lively duck

c. At home

d. We have

e. A beautiful horse

f. A curious cat

g. I have

h. I don't have

i. I would like to have

4. Sentence-level translation: Eng. to Cat.

a. My brother has a horse called Llampec.

b. My sister has an ugly turtle called George.

c. I have a fat hamster called Grassonet.

d. At home we have three pets: a duck, a rabbit and a parrot.

e. I have a rat called Stuart.

f. At home we have three pets: a cat, a dog and a hamster.

g. I have two fish called Nemo and Dory.

Unit 7. Talking about pets: WRITING

1. Split sentences

Tinc un gos que	blanca
A casa tenim	tenir una aranya
Tinc una rata	es diu Ringo
Tinc un gat	conillet d'Índies
M'agradaria	dues mascotes
El meu germà té un	casa
No tinc animals a	negre

2. Rewrite the sentences in the correct order

a. mascotes tenim A tres casa

b. rata una M'agradaria tenir

c. un Tinc gat un gos i

d. conill amic blanc El meu té Pau un

e. Fran verd un que Tenim es ocell diu

f. dos Tenim grocs peixos

g. té es diu germana un que La meva lloro Jack

3. Spot and correct the grammar and spelling. Note: in several cases a word is missing

a. A casa un gos un gat

b. Tinc un conillet d'Índies negra

c. agradaria tenir serp

d. meva germana tinc una gata blanca

e. El meu amic Pere té dos peix

f. El meu cavall em diu Rick

g. Tinc una cavall negre

h. A casa tenim dues mascota

4. Anagrams

a. ogs

b. tag

c. tara

d. ecàn

e. llocni

f. llacav

g. scomaast

6. Describe this person in the third person (he)

Name: Víctor

Hair: Blond, short

Eyes: Green

Personality: Very nice

Physical: Short

Pets: A dog, a cat and two fish and would like to have a spider

5. Guided writing: write 3 short paragraphs in the first person singular (I) describing the pets below

Name	Animal	Age	Colour	Character or appearance
Jan	Dog	4	White	Affectionate
Olivia	Duck	6	Blue	Funny
Maria	Horse	1	Brown	Beautiful

Grammar Time 3: TENIR (Part 2)
(Pets and description)

---

1. Translate into Catalan

a. I have: t _ _ _

b. You have: t _ _ _ _

c. She has: t _

d. We have: t _ _ _ _ _

e. You guys have: t _ _ _ _ _

f. They have: t _ _ _ _ _

---

2. Translate into English

a. Tinc un cavall preciós. Es diu Thor.

b. El meu germà té un gat molt lleig.

c. La meva mare té un gos molt divertit.

d. Els meus cosins tenen un conillet d'Índies molt grassonet.

e. A casa tenim un ànec molt sorollós.

f. El meu amic Xavi té una tortuga molt gran.

---

3. Complete

a. *I have a guinea pig*   T______________ un conillet d'Índies.

b. *It is two years old*   T________ dos anys.

c. *We have a turtle. It is 4 years old*   T______________ una tortuga. T________ quatre anys.

d. *My sister has a dog*   La meva germana t_______ un gos.

e. *My uncles have two cats*   Els meus tiets t____________ dos gats.

f. *They are three years old*   T______________ tres anys.

g. *My brother and I have a snake*   El meu germà i jo t______________ una serp.

h. *Do you guys have pets?*   T______________ mascotes?

i. *What animals do you have?*   Quins animals t____________?

---

4. Translate into Catalan

a. I have a monkey. It is three years old.

b. We don't have pets at home.

c. My dog is three years old. It is very big.

d. I have three brothers. They are very nice.

e. My cousins have a duck and a guinea pig.

f. My auntie has blond, curly and long hair. She is very pretty.

g. My brother and I have black hair and green eyes.

Question Skills 1: Age / Descriptions / Pets

1. Match question and answer

Quants anys tens?	Tenen vuitanta anys
Per què no et portes bé amb la teva mare?	Estic bé, gràcies
Com són els teus cabells?	Tinc quinze anys
Quants anys tenen els teus avis?	És el blau
De quin color són els teus ulls?	Perquè és molt estricta
Quin és el teu color preferit?	És el gos
Com estàs?	Soc simpàtic i parlador
Tens mascotes?	No, perquè és molt seriós i mandrós
Quin és el teu animal preferit?	El vint de juny
Quantes mascotes tens?	Són negres
Com ets de caràcter?	Són blaus
Com ets físicament?	En tinc dos. Un gat i un lloro
Et portes bé amb el teu pare?	No, no en tinc
Quan és el teu aniversari?	Soc baix i guapo

2. Complete with the missing words

a. D' _________ ets?
Where are you from?

b. _________ ets de caràcter?
What are you like in terms of character?

c. _________ anys té el teu pare?
How old is your father?

d. Et _________ bé amb la teva mare?
Do you get along with your mum?

e. _________ és el teu aniversari?
When is your birthday?

f. _________ és el teu gos?
What is your dog like?

g. _________ mascotes tens?
How many pets do you have?

3. Translate the following question words into English

a. Quin? _________________

b. Quan? _________________

c. On? _________________

d. Com? _________________

e. D'on? _________________

f. Qui? _________________

g. Quant? _________________

h. Quants? _________________

i. ¿Per què? _________________

5. Translate into Catalan

a. What is your name?

b. How old are you?

c. What is your hair like?

d. What is your favourite animal?

e. Do you get along with your father?

f. Why don't you get along with your mother?

g. How many pets do you have?

h. Where are you from?

4. Complete

a. Q_________ a_______ tens?

b. D'______ ets?

c. C_______ é__ el t_______ g_______?

d. C_____ e____ d_____?

e. Q________ m_________ tens?

f. Q______ anys t_______?

g. E__ p______ b__ a____ el t__ p______?

UNIT 8
Saying what jobs people do, why they like/dislike them and where they work

Grammar Time: -ar verbs like *treballar* + SER

In this unit will learn how to say:

- What jobs people do
- Why they like/dislike those jobs
- Where they work
- Adjectives to describe jobs
- Words for useful jobs
- Words for types of buildings
- The full conjugation of the verb 'Treballar' (to work) in the present indicative

You will revisit the following:
- Family members
- The full conjugation of the verb 'ser' (to be)
- Description of people and pets

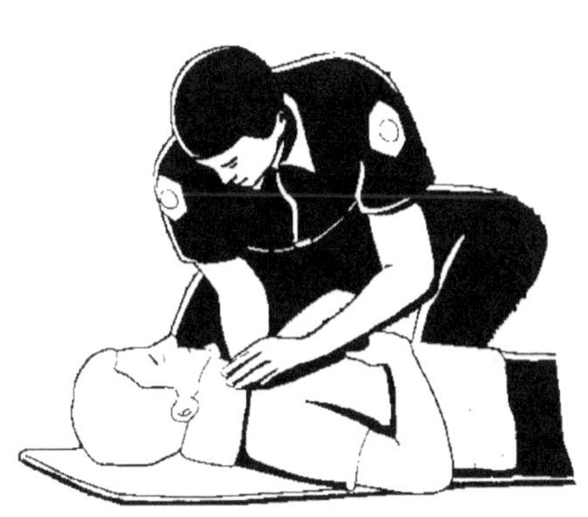

UNIT 8
Saying what jobs people do, why they like/dislike them and where they work

El meu germà petit *My younger brother*	**és** *he is*	**actor** *actor* **advocat** *lawyer* **comptable** *accountant* **cuiner** *chef* **enginyer** *engineer* **granger** *farmer*		**avorrit** *boring*	**Treballa a** *he/she works in* **(al) camp** *the countryside*
El meu pare *My father*	**treballa de/d'** *works as a*	**home de negocis** *business man* **infermer** *nurse* **mecànic** *mechanic* **mestre de casa** *house-husband* **metge** *doctor* **perruquer** *hairdresser* **professor** *teacher*	**li agrada perquè és** *he/she likes it because it is* **no li agrada perquè és** *he/she doesn't like it because it is*	**difícil** *difficult* **divertit** *funny* **emocionant** *exciting* **estimulant** *stimulating*	**casa** *at home* **la ciutat** *the city* **Treballa en** *he/she works in* **una empresa** *a company* **una escola** *a school* **un garatge** *a garage*
El meu tiet *My uncle*					
La meva germana gran *My older sister*	**és** *she is*	**actriu** *actress* **advocada** *lawyer* **comptable** *accountant* **cuinera** *chef* **dona de negocis** *business woman* **enginyera** *engineer* **grangera** *farmer*	**li encanta perquè és** *he/she loves it because it is*	**estressant** *stressful* **fàcil** *easy*	**una granja** *a farm* **un hotel** *a hotel* **una oficina** *an office*
La meva mare *My mother*	**treballa de/d'** *works as a*	**infermera** *nurse* **mecànica** *mechanic* **mestressa de casa** *house-wife* **metgessa** *doctor* **perruquera** *hairdresser* **professora** *teacher*	**ho odia perquè és** *he/she hates it because it is*	**gratificant** *rewarding* **interessant** *interesting*	**un restaurant** *a restaurant* **un taller** *a workshop* **un teatre** *a theatre*
La meva tieta *My aunt*					

Unit 8. Saying what jobs people do: VOCABULARY BUILDING

1. Complete with the missing word

a. El meu pare és _____________. *My father is a lawyer.*

b. La meva tieta és _______________. *My aunt is a hairdresser.*

c. El meu germà petit treballa com a _______________.
My younger brother works as a mechanic.

d. La meva mare és _______________. *My mother is a doctor.*

e. La meva germana _______________ treballa com a
_______________. *My older sister works as an engineer.*

f. La meva tieta és _____________. *My aunt is an accountant.*

g. El meu _______ és _____________. *My uncle is a farmer.*

2. Match

és avorrit	it's stressful
no és avorrit	it's fun
és difícil	it's hard
és divertit	it's not boring
és emocionant	it's rewarding
és estressant	it's boring
és fàcil	it's interesting
és gratificant	it's easy
és interessant	it's exciting

3. Translate into English

a. La meva mare és mecànica

b. Li agrada la seva feina (*job*)

c. Treballa en un garatge

d. El meu germà és comptable

e. No li agrada la seva feina

f. El meu cosí és perruquer

g. Li encanta la seva feina

h. Perquè és divertit

4. Add the missing letter

a. És f_cil

b. L_ agrada

c. Engin_era

d. Met_e

e. És etres_ant

f. Tr_balla com a

g. És _nfermer

h. El meu ti_t

5. Anagrams

a. jerGran

b. atvocAd

c. geMetssa

d. riutcA

e. roAct

f. Comblepta

g. Perreruqu

h. nercui

6. Broken words

a. É___ m_________ d__ c_________   *He is a house husband*

b. L__ a_________ la s_________ f_________   *He likes his job*

c. El m____ g_________ é___ g_________   *My bro is a farmer*

d. T_____________   *He/she works*

e. Al c_____________   *In the countryside*

f. O________ la s_____ f_________   *He hates his job*

g. P_________ é__ a_________   *Because it is boring*

h. É___ m_____ g_____________   *It is very rewarding*

7. Complete with a suitable word

a. La meva mare és _____________

b. Li _________ la seva feina

c. Li agrada perquè és ___________

d. Treballa a _____________

e. El meu _________ és perruquer

f. No _____ agrada la seva feina

g. Perquè és molt _____________

h. La m_______ tieta és metgessa

i. Li agrada la seva _________

j. El meu tiet és mecànic, treballa a
un _____________

Unit 8. Saying what jobs people do: READING

Em dic Arnau. Tinc vint anys i visc a Andorra. A la meva família hi ha quatre persones. Tinc un gos molt divertit, el Felip. El meu pare treballa com a metge, a la ciutat. Li agrada la seva feina perquè és gratificant i divertida. El meu tiet Dani és granger i li encanta la seva feina. A vegades és una feina dura i difícil, però li encanten els animals.
Arnau. 20 anys, Andorra

Em dic Sebastià. A la meva família hi ha quatre persones. El meu pare es diu Mateu i és advocat. Li agrada la seva feina perquè és interessant. Encara que a vegades és estressant. La meva mare és mestressa de casa i li agrada bastant la seva feina. Diu que és molt gratificant. Tinc un gos que es diu Dog. És molt gran i divertit! No m'agraden els gats.
Sebastià. 15 anys, Eivissa

Em dic Samuel. Visc a València. La meva persona preferida és la meva mare. És tímida però molt simpàtica. La meva mare és enginyera però ara no treballa. Odio al meu tiet, és intel·ligent però molt antipàtic. El meu tiet és professor però odia la seva feina perquè és difícil i avorrida. Treballa en una escola a València, però odia als nens. A casa tinc una tortuga que es diu Spiderman. És lenta però molt graciosa, igual que la meva germana Marina.
Samuel. 9 anys, València

Em dic Clara. A la meva família hi ha quatre persones. La meva mare es diu Valeria i és perruquera. Li agrada la seva feina perquè és interessant. El meu pare és mestre de casa però no li agrada molt la seva feina perquè diu que és molt difícil i una mica avorrida. A casa no tinc un animal però m'agradaria tenir un cavall. El meu cosí te un cavall que es diu David, és molt gran i fort. Què guai!
Clara. 12 anys, Cerdanyola del Vallès

1. Find the Catalan in Arnau's text

a. I am 20

b. I have a dog

c. my dad works as…

d. a doctor

e. in the city

f. he likes his work

g. it is rewarding

h. sometimes

i. he loves his work

2. Answer the questions below about all texts

a. Who is David?

b. Whose mum is a housewife?

c. Who has an uncle that is in the wrong job?

d. Whose father is a doctor?

e. Who has a turtle?

f. Who has a dog?

3. Answer the following questions about Samuel

a. Where does Samuel live?

b. Who is his favourite person?

c. What does his mum do? (2 details)

d. Why does he hate his uncle?

e. Why is his uncle a bad teacher?

f. Who is Spiderman?

g. What is Marina like?

4. Fill in the blanks

Em d______ Neus. Tinc tretze a________ i v_________ a Tarragona. A la meva f_________ hi ha cinc persones. El meu cosí Jordi é____ molt parlador i amable, té trenta anys. El Jordi és pr___________ i treballa en una e_________. Viu a Liverpool, a Anglaterra. Li agrada la seva f_________ perquè és int_________. El meu pa_____ no treballa ara. A casa tinc u___ animal que es d___ Damià. És una ara____: una taràntula!

5. Fill in the table below

Name	Neus	Jordi
Age		
City		
Pets/Job		
Opinion of job	–	

Unit 8. Saying what jobs people do: TRANSLATION

1. Faulty translation: spot and correct (in the English) the translation mistakes

a. El meu pare treballa com a actor i li agrada molt perquè és emocionant. Treballa en un teatre.
My father works as a cook and he really likes his job because it is interesting. He works in a school.

b. La meva tieta treballa com a dona de negocis en una oficina. Li agrada però és dur.
My aunt works as a business woman in a hair salon. She hates it but it's hard.

c. El meu amic Fran treballa com a infermer. Treballa en un hospital i li agrada la seva feina.
My enemy Fran works as a nurse. He lives in a hospital and likes his work.

d. El meu tiet Gianfranco és cuiner en un restaurant italià i li encanta. *My uncle Gianfranco is a lawyer in an Italian restroom and he likes it.*

e. La meva àvia Emilia és comptable i treballa en una oficina. Odia la seva feina perquè és avorrida i repetitiva. *My mother Emilia is an actress and works in an office. She loves her work because it is boring and repetitive.*

3. Phrase-level translation: English to Catalan

a. my big brother

b. works as

c. farmer

d. he likes

e. his job

f. because it's interesting

g. and fun

h. but it's tough

2. Translate into English

a. El meu tiet treballa de

b. El meu pare treballa com a

c. Mestre de casa

d. Infermera

e. Perruquer

f. Mecànic

g. Li encanta la seva feina

h. Treballa en un taller

i. Treballa en un teatre

j. Treballa en un garatge

k. És gratificant

l. És dur però divertit

4. Sentence-level translation: Eng. to Cat.

a. My brother is a mechanic

b. My father is a businessman

c. My uncle is a farmer and hates his job

d. My brother Dídac works in a restaurant

e. At home I have a snake

f. I have a fun dog and a mean cat

g. My aunt is a nurse. She likes her job…

h. …because it is rewarding

i. My aunt works in a hospital

Unit 8. Saying what jobs people do: WRITING

1. Split sentences

El meu germà té	interessant
La meva tieta és	com a advocat
El meu cosí treballa	professora
Li agrada	un restaurant
Perquè és	empresa
Treballa en	la seva feina
Treballa en una	un ànec negre

2. Rewrite the sentences in the correct order

a. Li feina la seva agrada

b. de comptable Treballa en una oficina

c. li agrada És de casa i mestre

d. El meu granger treballa com a tiet

e. en un teatre germà El meu treballa

f. El meu odia la feina seva avi

g. El meu hospital treballa en un amic i és metge

3. Spot and correct the grammar and spelling

a. La meva mare és mestresso de casa

b. És un feina avorrida i difícil

c. La meva germana treballa com a perruquer

d. Ella odia la seva feina perquè és dura i repetitiu

e. Treballa en una hospital a ciutat

f. Li agrado molt la seva feina perquè és fàcil

g. El meu para odia la seva feina

h. Li agrada la seva feina perquè és gratificants

4. Anagrams

a. geteM

b. Gratantific

c. Ritipeteu

d. iL adagra

e. janaGr

f. taurResant

g. Pssorrofe

5. Guided writing: write 3 short paragraphs in the first person singular (I) describing the people below

Person	Relation	Job	Like/ Dislike	Reason
Jordi	My dad	Mechanic	Loves	Interesting
Oriol	My brother	Lawyer	Hates	Boring and repetitive
Marta	My aunt	Farmer	Likes	Tough but fun

6. Describe this person in the third person (she)

Name: Magda

Hair: Blond + green eyes

Physique: Tall and slim

Personality: Hard-working

Job: Nurse

Opinion: Likes her job a lot

Reason: Stressful but rewarding

Grammar Time 4: The present indicative of
Treballar and other –ar verbs

Jo	**treballo** *I work*		**advocat/advocada** *lawyer*
Tu	**treballes** *you work*		**comptable** *accountant*
Ell **El meu germà** **El meu pare**	**treballa** *he works*		**cuiner/a** *chef* **dependent/a** *shop assistant* **dona de negocis** *businesswoman*
Ella **La meva germana** **La meva mare**	**treballa** *she works*	**com a** (as)	**enginyer/a** *engineer* **granger/a** *farmer* **home de negocis** *businessman* **infermer/a** *nurse*
Nosaltres **El meu pare i jo**	**treballem** *we work*		**mecànic/a** *mechanic* **mestre de casa** *house-husband*
Vosaltres	**treballeu** *you guys work*		**mestressa de casa** *house- wife*
Ells	**treballen** *they work*		**metge/metgessa** *doctor* **perruquer/a** *hairdresser*
Elles **Les meves germanes**	**treballen** *they work*		**professor/a** *teacher*

Drills

1. Match

Treballa	I work
Treballo	You work
Treballen	S/he works
Treballeu	We work
Treballem	You guys work
Treballes	They work

2. Translate into English

a. Treballo a vegades

b. Els meus pares treballen molt

c. El meu germà i jo no treballem

d. Ella no treballa mai

e. Treballes com a bomber?

f. Vosaltres treballeu en una botiga?

3. Complete with the correct option

a. El meu germà ____________ com a perruquer

b. Els meus pares no ________________

c. La meva germana i jo no ______________

d. La meva novia ____________ com a pilot

e. Els meus avis no ________________

f. (vosaltres) ______________ com a policies?

g. Perquè (tu) no __________________?

h. (jo) No ______________ encara

treballem	treballa	treballen	treballes
treballen	treballa	treballeu	treballo

<table>
<tr><td colspan="3">

4. Cross out the wrong option

</td></tr>
</table>

	A	B
Ells	treballen	treballeu
El meu germà	treballes	treballa
El meu pare	treballa	treballo
Els meus tiets	treballeu	treballen
Elles	treballen	treballem
Tu i jo	treballem	treballeu
Nosaltres	treballem	treballen
Vosaltres	treballa	treballeu
Els cosins	treballen	treballeu
Jo i ella	treballem	treballen

5. Complete the verbs

a. El meu germà i jo no treball __ __

b. Els meus pares no treball __ __

c. El meu pare treball __ com a advocat

d. Els meus germans no treball __ __

e. Tu treball __ __ molt

f. La meva mare treball __ a casa

g. Els meus tiets treball __ __ com a cuiners

h. La meva novia treball __ a una tenda

i. Vosaltres no treball__ __ mai!

6. Complete with the correct form of *treballar*

a. Els meus pares _________________ com a obrers   *My parents work as workers*

b. La meva mare _______________ de professora   *My mother works as a teacher*

c. Els meus pares ______________ com a comptables   *My parents work as accountants*

d. El meu pare _______________ com a periodista   *My father works as a journalist*

e. El meu germà no ___________________   *My brother doesn't work*

f. Les meves germanes tampoc __________________   *My sisters don't work either*

g. El meu tiet ________________ de bomber   *My uncle works as a fireman*

h. Els meus cosins i jo no __________________   *My cousins and I don't work*

i. (jo) _______________ a un restaurant   *I work in a restaurant*

j. La meva novia ____________ en una botiga de roba   *My girlfriend works in a clothing store*

k. On ________________ ?   *Where do you work?*

Verbs like TREBALLAR

Adorar: to love

Sopar: to have dinner

Esmorzar: to eat for breakfast

Escoltar: to listen to

Estudiar: to study

Parlar: to speak

Practicar: to practise

Tocar: to play (an instrument)

Jugar: to play (games or sports)

7. Complete the sentences using the correct form of the verbs in the grey box on the left

a. Ador__   als meus avis   *I love my grandparents*

b. Esmorz___ cereals   *He has cereals for breakfast*

c. Practic_______ el català   *I practise Catalan*

d. Parl___ anglès?   *Do you speak English?*

e. On sop___ ?   *Where do you have dinner?*

f. Toqu_____ la guitarra?   *Do you guys play the guitar?*

g. Escolt___ música rock   *I listen to rock music*

h. Mai jug___ a futbol   *I never play football*

Grammar Time 5: SER (Part 2)
(Present indicative of *ser* and jobs)

Present Indicative of *ser*		Jobs (nouns)	
		Singular	Plural
MASCULINE			
Jo	**soc** *I am*	actor	actors
Tu	**ets** *you are*	advocat	advocats
		comptable	comptables
Ell El meu germà El meu pare	**és** *he is*	cuiner dependent enginyer	cuiners dependents enginyers
Nosaltres El meu pare i jo	**som** *we are*	granger infermer	grangers infermers
Vosaltres	**sou** *you are (plural)*	mecànic mestre de casa	mecànics mestres de casa
Ells Els meus germans Els meus pares	**són** *they are*	metge perruquer professor	metges perruquers professors
FEMININE			
Jo	**soc** *I am*	actriu	actrius
Tu	**ets** *are*	advocada	advocades
		comptable	comptables
Ella La meva germana La meva mare	**és** *she is*	cuinera dependenta enginyera	cuineres dependentes enginyeres
Nosaltres La meva mare i jo	**som** *we are*	grangera infermera	grangeres infermeres
Vosaltres	**sou** *you are (plural)*	mecànica mestressa de casa	mecàniques mestresses de casa
Elles Les meves germanes Les meves tietes	**són** *they are*	metgessa perruquera professora	metgesses perruqueres professores

Drills

1. Match

Soc	She/he is
Som	You are
Són	We are
Ets	I am
És	They are
Sou	You guys are

3. Translate into English

a. Som perruquers

b. Són policies

c. Ets bomber?

d. La Maria és model

e. Són obrers en una obra *(building site)*

f. Soc policia

g. Sou infermers?

h. Som metgesses

i. El meu pare i jo som actors

j. Sou professores?

k. Soc granger

2. Complete with the missing forms of *ser*

a. La meva mare i jo __________ metgesses

b. Els meus germans __________ obrers

c. La meva germana __________ infermera

d. Els meus pares i jo __________ jardiners

e. (tu) __________ advocada?

f. (jo) __________ bombera

g. (ells) No __________ policies

h. (vosaltres) __________ models?

i. (vosaltres) __________ actrius, veritat?

j. Els meus tiets __________ cantants famosos

4. Translate into Catalan (easier)

a. My mother is a doctor

b. My parents are policemen

c. My aunt is a lawyer

d. I am a teacher

e. My cousins *(m)* are mechanics

f. My uncle is a singer

g. My friend Josep is an actor

5. Translate into Catalan (harder)

a. My brother is tall and handsome. He is an actor.

b. My older sister is very intelligent and hard-working. She is a scientist.

c. My younger brother is very sporty. He works at a gym.

d. My mother is hard-working. She is a doctor.

e. My father is very patient, calm and organized. He is a teacher.

UNIT 9
Comparing people's appearance and personality

In this unit will learn how to say in Catalan:
- More/less ... than
- As ... as
- New adjectives to describe people

You will revisit the following:
- Family members
- Pets
- Describing animals' appearance and character

Jo			**afectuós/a** *affectionate*		jo
Ell			**alt/a** *tall*		tu
Ella			**amable** *kind*		ell / ella
El meu avi			**antipàtic/a** *unfriendly*		ells / elles
La meva àvia			**avorrit/avorrida** *boring*		el meu avi
El meu amic		**més** *more*	**baix/a** *short*	**que** *than*	la meva àvia
La meva amiga			**dèbil** *weak*		els meus avis
El meu millor amic	**soc** *am*		**divertit/divertida** *funny*		el meu amic
La meva millor amiga			**esportista** *sporty*		la meva amiga
			estúpid/a *stupid*		els meus amics
El meu germà			**fort/a** *strong*		el meu germà
La meva germana			**gras/grassa** *fat*		la meva germana
El meu fill			**guapo/a** *good-looking*		els meus germans
La meva filla		**menys** *less*	**intel·ligent** *intelligent*	**que** *than*	el meu fill
El meu pare			**jove** *young*		la meva filla
La meva mare			**lleig/lletja** *ugly*		els meus fills
El meu cosí			**mandrós/a** *lazy*		el meu pare
La meva cosina			**parlador/a** *talkative*		la meva mare
El meu tiet	**és** *is*		**prim/a** *slim*		els meus pares
La meva tieta			**seriós/a** *serious*		el meu cosí
El meu xicot			**simpàtic/a** *nice*		la meva cosina
La meva xicota		**tan** *as*	**sorollós/a** *noisy*	**com** *as*	els meus cosins
El meu ànec			**tranquil/·la** *relaxed, calm*		el meu tiet
El meu gat			**treballador/a** *hard-working*		la meva tieta
El meu gos			**vell/a** *old*		els meus tiets
La meva iguana					el meu xicot
La meva tortuga					la meva xicota
					el meu gat
					el meu gos
					la meva tortuga

Unit 9. Comparing people : VOCABULARY BUILDING

1. Complete with the missing word

a. El meu pare és més alt _______ el meu germà gran — *My father is taller than my older brother*

b. La meva mare és ______ parladora que la meva _________ — *My mother is less talkative than my aunt*

c. El meu _______ és més baix que el _____ pare — *My grandfather is shorter than my dad*

d. Els meus cosins són ______ mandrosos que ____________ — *My cousins are lazier than us*

e. El meu gos _____ més ___________ que el meu ________ — *My dog is more noisy than my cat*

f. La meva tieta és ______ guapa que la _______ mare — *My aunt is less pretty than my mother*

g. El meu ___________ és més _________________ que jo — *My bro is more hard-working than me*

h. Els meus pares _____ més ___________ que els meus tiets — *My parents are more kind than my uncles*

i. El meu germà petit és _________ alt ________ jo — *My younger brother is as tall as me*

2. Translate into English

a. els meus cosins

b. més

c. el meu tiet

d. els meus avis

e. la meva germana

f. el meu millor amic

g. treballador

h. la meva amiga

i. alt

j. vell

k. tossut

l. mandrós

3. Match

treballador	strong
guapo	serious
amable	sporty
fort	good-looking
esportista	old
vell	hard-working
seriós	kind

4. Correct the translation mistakes

a. És més alt que jo — *He is taller than you*

b. És tan guapo como jo — *He is as funny as me*

c. És més tranquil·la que jo — *She is stronger than me*

d. Soc menys gras que ell — *I am more fat than him*

e. Són menys baixos que tu — *They are shorter than us*

f. Soc tan vell com ell — *She is as old as him*

g. És més esportista que jo — *You are more sporty than me*

5. Complete with a suitable word

a. La meva mare és ______ alta ______ jo

b. El ____ pare ____ més jove que el meu tiet

c. Els meus pares són ______ alts com els ______ avis

d. Els ______ germans ________ més esportistes que jo

e. El meu ________ és menys sorollós _________ el meu gos

f. Els meus avis _______ tan afectuosos _______ els meus pares

g. La meva novia és ________ guapa que la ______ tortuga

h. El meu tiet no ____ tan fort _________ el meu ____________

6. Match the opposites

guapo	baix
treballador	avorrit
jove	lleig
alt	gras
divertit	menys
dèbil	mandrós
més	vell
prim	fort

Unit 9. Comparing people : READING

Em dic Jordi. Tinc vint anys i visc a Dénia. A la meva família som cinc persones: jo, els meus pares i els meus dos germans, el Ferran i l'Àlex. El Ferran és més alt, guapo i fort que l'Àlex, però l'Àlex és més amable, intel·ligent i treballador que el Ferran.

Els meus pares es diuen Antoni i Núria. Els dos són molt amables, però el meu pare és més estricte que la meva mare. A més, la meva mare és més pacient i menys tossuda que el meu pare. I jo soc tan tossut com el meu pare! A casa tenim dues mascotes: una tortuga i un ànec. Els dos són molt simpàtics, però l'ànec és més sorollós. Tan sorollós com jo.

Jordi, 20 anys. Dénia

Em dic Josep. Tinc quinze anys i visc a Manacor. A la meva família som cinc persones: els meus pares, els meus dos germans, Robert i Pere, i jo. El Robert és més prim i més esportista que el Pere, però el Pere és més alt i fort.

Els meus pares es diuen Carmen i Rafael. Prefereixo al meu pare, perquè és menys estricte que la meva mare. A més, la meva mare és més tossuda que el meu pare. Jo soc tan tossut com ella! A casa tenim dues mascotes: un lloro i un conillet d'Índies. Els dos són molt simpàtics, però el lloro és molt més parlador, tan parlador com jo.

Josep, 15 anys. Manacor

Em dic Victòria. Tinc vint anys i visc a Figueres amb els meus pares i les meves dues germanes, la Marina i la Vero. La Marina és més guapa que la Vero, però la Vero és més simpàtica.

Els meus pares són molt afectuosos i amables, però el meu pare és més divertit que la meva mare. Jo soc tan graciosa com el meu pare! A casa tenim dues mascotes: un gos i un conill. Els dos són molt grassos, però el gos és més mandrós. Tan mandrós com jo. **Victòria, 20 anys. Figueres**

---

1. Find the Catalan for the following in Jordi's text

a. I live in:

b. My parents:

c. Good-looking:

d. Hard-working:

e. Less stubborn:

f. More patient:

g. But:

h. Duck:

i. Two pets:

j. Very nice:

k. As stubborn as:

2. Complete the statements below based on Victòria's text

a. I am _______ years old

b. Marina is more _______ than Vero

c. Vero is more _______

d. My parents are very _________ and _______

e. I am as _____________ as my father

f. We have _______ pets: a _____ and a ___________

---

3. Correct any incorrect statements about Josep's text

a. El Josep té tres mascotes

b. El Robert és més gras que el Pere

c. El Robert és més dèbil que el Pere

d. El Josep és tan parlador com el seu conillet d'Índies

e. El Josep prefereix a la seva mare

4. Answer the questions below about all three texts

a. Where does Josep live?

b. Who is stricter, his mother or his father?

c. Who is as talkative as their parrot?

d. Who is as chatty as their duck?

e. Who has a stubborn father?

f. Who has a rabbit?

g. Who has a guinea pig?

h. Which one of Josep's brothers is sportier?

i. What are the differences between Jordi's brothers?

Unit 9. Comparing people: TRANSLATION/WRITING

<table>
<tr><td valign="top" width="50%">

1. Translate into English

a. Alt

b. Prim

c. Baix

d. Gras

e. Intel·ligent

f. Tossut

g. Estúpid

h. Guapo

i. Lleig

j. Més ... que

k. Menys ... que

l. Fort

m. Dèbil

n. Tan ... com ...

</td><td valign="top" width="50%">

2. Complete with the missing words

a. La meva __________ és ______ alta ______ la meva tieta

My mother is taller than my aunt

b. El _____ pare _____ més _____ que el meu germà gran

My father is stronger than my older brother

c. Els meus __________ són menys _____________ que nosaltres

My cousins are less sporty than us

d. El _____ germà és _______ tranquil que ________

My brother is calmer than me

e. La meva mare _____ _______ amable ________ el meu pare

My mother is as kind as my father

f. La meva ___________ és ______ treballadora que ____________

My sister is more hard-working than us

g. La meva __________ és menys ____________ ______ jo

My girlfriend is less serious than me

h. El meu ______ és ________ tossut ______ la meva àvia

My grandfather is more stubborn than my grandmother

</td></tr>
<tr><td valign="top">

3. Phrase-level translation: Eng. to Cat.

a. My mother is

b. Taller *(f)* than

c. As slim *(f)* as

d. Less stubborn *(f)* than

e. I am shorter *(m)* than

f. My parents are

g. My cousins are

h. As handsome as

i. They are as smart as

j. My grandparents are

k. I am as lazy *(f)* as

</td><td valign="top">

4. Sentence-level translation: Eng. to Cat.

a. My older sister is taller than my mother.

b. My father is as stubborn as my mother.

c. My girlfriend is more hard-working than me.

d. I am more intelligent than my dog.

e. My best friend is sportier than me.

f. My boyfriend is better-looking than me.

g. Our cousins are uglier than us.

h. My duck is noisier than my dog.

i. My cat is funnier than my turtle.

j. My rabbit is less fat than my guinea pig.

</td></tr>
</table>

Revision Quickie 2 : Family, Pets and Jobs

1. Match

Obrer	Doctor
Advocat	Waiter
Infermer	Journalist
Cambrer	Nurse
Periodista	IT worker
Metge	Worker
Hostessa	Air hostess
Bomber	Lawyer
Informàtic	Firefighter

2. Categories: sort the words below in the categories

a. obrer; b. alt; c. granger; d. graciós; e. baix; f. cosí;
g. professora; h. infermer; i. tiet; j. pare ; k. blau; l. gras; m. guapo;
n. bombera; o. mare; p. germà; q. conill; r. castany; s. ànec; t. gat

Descripcions	Animals	Professions	Família

3. Complete with the missing adjectives

a. El meu pare és ______________ *funny*

b. La meva mare és ___________ *tall*

c. El meu germà és ___________ *short*

d. La meva novia és ___________ *pretty*

e. El meu cosí és ______________ *fun*

f. El meu profe d'anglès és ________ *boring*

4. Complete with the missing nouns

a. El meu pare treballa com a _________ *lawyer*

b. La meva mare és _______________ *nurse*

c. El meu millor amic és ______________ *journalist*

d. La meva germana és _______________ *air hostess*

e. El meu cosí és __________________ *student*

f. Jo treballo com a _________________ *doctor*

g. La Marta és __________________ *politician*

h. La meva àvia és __________________ *singer*

5. Match the opposites

Alt	Treballador
Guapo	Estúpid
Gras	Baix
Mandrós	Silenciós
Intel·ligent	Lleig
Sorollós	Impacient
Dolent	Prim
Pacient	Bo

6. Complete the numbers below

a. Cato_ _ _   14

b. Quara_ _ _   40

c. Seixa_ _ _   60

d. Cinqu_ _ _ _   50

e. Setan_ _   70

f. Nora_ _ _   90

7. Complete with the correct verb

a. La meva mare ___ alta. *My mother is tall*

b. ___________ els cabells negres. *I have black hair*

c. ____________ de granger. *I work as a farmer*

d. El meu pare ________ quaranta anys. *My father is 40*

e. Quantes persones ______ ______ a la teva família?
How many people are there in your family?

f. Els meus germans ______ alts. *My brothers are tall*

g. El meu germà no ______________
My brother doesn't work

h. La meva novia ___ ________ Elena
My girlfriend is called Elena

UNIT 10
Saying what's in my school bag / classroom / Describing colour

Grammar Time: verb *tenir* & Agreements

In this unit you will learn how to say:
- What objects you have in your schoolbag/pencil case/classroom
- Words for classroom equipment
- What you have and don't have

You will revisit the following:
- Colours
- How adjectives agree in gender and number with nouns
- Introducing yourself (e.g. name, age, town, country)
- Pets

UNIT 10.
Saying what's in my school bag / classroom
Describing colour

A la meva motxilla *In my schoolbag*		A la meva classe *In my class*
Hi ha / No hi ha *There is / There isn't*	**un bolígraf** *a pen*	blanc
	un diccionari *a dictionary*	blau
	un estoig *a pencil case*	gris
	un llapis *a pencil*	groc
	un llibre *a book*	negre
Tinc / No tinc *I have / I don't have*	**un ordinador** *a computer*	rosa
	un paper *a paper*	taronja
	un quadern *an exercise book*	verd
	un regle *a ruler*	vermell
Em fa falta / Necessito *I need*	**un retolador** *a felt tip pen*	
	uns bolígrafs *some pens*	grocs
	uns llapis *some pencils*	marrons
No em fa falta / **No necessito** *I don't need*	**uns retoladors** *some felt tip pens*	taronges
	una agenda *a planner*	blanca
	una cadira *a chair*	blava
	una calculadora *a calculator*	grisa
El meu amic Fran té *My friend Fran has*	**cola** *gluestick*	groga
	una goma *a rubber*	rosa
	una pissarra *a whiteboard*	taronja negra
	una taula *a table*	vermella
El meu amic Fran no té *My friend Fran does not have*	**una maquineta** *a pencil sharpener*	
	estisores *scissors*	grogues

Unit 10. Saying what's in my school bag: VOCABULARY BUILDING

1. Complete with the missing word

a. Tinc un ____________   *I have a book*

b. Em fa falta una ________   *I need an eraser*

c. No tinc cap ____________   *I don't have any pen*

d. El meu amic _____un paper   *My friend has a paper*

e. Tinc ____ calculadora   *I have a calculator*

f. Em fa falta una _________   *I need a chair*

g. No tinc cap __________   *I don't have any ruler*

h. El meu amic té ___________   *My friend has scissors*

2. Match

una goma	a pencil
un llapis	a planner
una agenda	I have a
una cadira	a sharpener
tinc un	a pen
necessito	I don't have
no tinc	a chair
una maquineta	a rubber
un bolígraf	I need

3. Translate into English

a. Tinc una goma

b. El meu amic té una agenda

c. No tinc un quadern

d. Tinc un llapis

e. No tinc una maquineta

f. Em fa falta un retolador

g. Hi ha un ordinador

h. No tinc un retolador

4. Add the missing letter

a. Una maquine_a   e. Una _genda

b. Una g_ma   f. El meu ami__

c. Em f_ falta   g. No t_

d. No t_nc   h. Una pi__ _arra

5. Anagrams

a. isLlap *Llapis*   e. sotiEsres

b. Eigtos   f. xiMollat

c. ronTaja   g. maGo

d. Blcan   h. rdVe

6. Broken words

a. A l__ m_______ m__________ t_________ u__ e____________
In my bag I have a pencil case

b. Al m___ e____________ t_________ alguns l____________
In my pencil case I have some pencils

c. N__ t__________ cap g________   *I don't have an/any eraser*

d. E__ f___ f__________ u__ r________   *I need a ruler*

e. H__ h__ u_____ p______________   *There is a whiteboard*

f. T______ alguns b__________ b________   *I have some blue pens*

g. N______________ u__ r___________   *I need a felt tip pen*

7. Complete with a suitable word

a. Tinc un ____________

b. Em ____ falta un llapis

c. M'agrada el color ___________

d. _______ un ordinador

e. Un llapis ____________

f. Una __________ vermella

g. La meva __________ té un estoig

h. No _______ cap regle

i. Ell no ____ un retolador groc

j. Uns llapis ____________

k. Hi ____ una pissarra

Unit 10. Saying what's in my school bag: READING

Em dic Bruna. Tinc dotze anys i visc a Milà, a Itàlia. A la meva família hi ha quatre persones. Tinc un gat blanc. A la meva motxilla tinc moltes coses. Tinc un llapis vermell, un bolígraf groc, un regle vermell i una goma blanca. És la meva goma preferida. La meva amiga només té una cosa al seu estoig, un llapis. Però a casa seva té un cavall gris!
Bruna, 12 anys. Milà

Em dic Andrea. Tinc quinze anys i visc a Edimburg, a Escòcia. A la meva família hi ha tres persones. Tinc un conillet d'Índies molt divertit. A la meva classe hi ha moltes coses. Hi ha una pissarra, un ordinador i trenta taules. La meva classe és molt gran. Tinc un llapis blau, un retolador groc, un regle nou i una goma. El meu amic Martí té llapis de tots els colors.
Andrea, 15 anys. Edimburg

Em dic Gonzalo. Tinc divuit anys i visc a Cadis, a Espanya. A la meva família hi ha cinc persones. La meva germana es diu Montserrat. A la meva classe hi ha una pissarra i vint taules. També hi ha vint cadires, una per cada persona. La meva classe és bonica i el meu professor és molt divertit. Però no tinc cap llapis, cap bolígraf, cap regle ni cap goma. No tinc res. Em fa falta tot. A casa tinc una rata blanca molt graciosa. **Gonzalo, 18 anys. Cadis**

Em dic Emili. Tinc onze anys i visc a Ciutat de Mèxic, la capital de Mèxic. A la meva família hi ha quatre persones. M'encanta la meva mare però no m'agrada el meu pare. Ell és advocat. A la meva classe no hi ha moltes coses. No hi ha ni una pissarra ni un ordinador. Hi ha vint-i-vuit taules, però només hi ha vint-i-set cadires. És un problema! Tinc un llapis, una calculadora i una agenda. **Emili, 11. Mèxic**

1. Find the Catalan for the following in Bruna's text

a. I am 12

b. I live in Milan

c. there are 4 people

d. a white cat

e. a red pencil

f. a yellow pen

g. it is my favourite rubber

h. only has one thing

i. in her house

j. a grey horse

2. Find someone who

a. ...has a blue pencil

b. ...has most tables in their class

c. ...has a class with one student always standing

d. ...has no school equipment

e. ...has a big pet

f. ...doesn't like their dad

3. Answer the following questions about Gonzalo

a. Where does Gonzalo live?

b. Who is Montserrat?

c. How many tables and chairs are there in his class?

d. How does he describe his class?

e. What school equipment does he have?

f. What pet does he have?

g. How does he describe his pet?

5. Fill in the blanks

Em d________ José Luis. Tinc vuit a________ i v_________ a Sant Sebastià, al País Basc. A la meva família h__ h___ quatre persones. A c________ meva hi ha moltes coses, com un ordinador ___ una p___________. Al meu e_________ tinc un l________, un bolígraf b_______ i una g_____. El meu ami__ té molts lla______ , però no té cap g_____. El meu professor de francès m'a________ molt perquè és molt sim__________.

4. Fill in the table below

Name	Bruna	Andrea
Age		
City		
Items in pencil case		

Unit 10. Saying what's in my school bag: TRANSLATION

1. Faulty translation: spot and correct (in the English) the translation mistakes

a. A la meva classe hi ha dues pissarres i un ordinador. El meu professor no m'agrada. – *In my class there is a whiteboard and a computer. I like my teacher.*

b. No tinc moltes coses al meu estoig. Tinc un llapis rosa, però no tinc un regle. – *I have many things in my pencil case. I have a red pencil but I don't have an eraser.*

c. A la família del meu amic Emili hi ha quatre persones. Necessita un retolador negre i una agenda. – *There are five people in my friend Emili's family. He needs a black pen and a diary.*

d. Necessito una maquineta i cola. No tinc cap regle. M'encanta el meu professor! – *I need paper and a rubber. I don't have any ruler. I hate my teacher!*

e. A la meva classe hi ha trenta taules i trenta cadires. Necessito una agenda, però tinc un diccionari. – *In my class there are thirty cats and thirty chairs. I need a pen but I have a dog.*

2. Translate into English

a. Necessito un

b. Tinc un llapis negre

c. Tinc un bolígraf blau

d. Un regle verd

e. Tinc un gos a casa

f. El meu amic té un llibre

g. El meu pare treballa com a

h. M'agrada el meu professor

i. Uns llapis grocs

j. Una pissarra gran

k. Tinc moltes coses

l. No tinc una maquineta

m. Em fa falta un diccionari

3. Phrase-level translation: English to Catalan

a. A red book

b. A black calculator

c. I don't have

d. I need

e. I like

f. There are

g. I have

h. My friend has

4. Sentence-level translation: Eng. to Cat.

a. There are 20 tables

b. There is a whiteboard

c. My teacher *(masc.)* is nice

d. I have some blue pens

e. I have some orange pencils

f. I need an eraser and a sharpener

g. I need a chair and a book

h. My class is very big and pretty

i. My father is a teacher

Unit 10. Saying what's in my school bag: WRITING

1. Split sentences

Tinc una	té cap llapis
Em fa	agrada
La meva classe	falta un llapis
Hi ha trenta	calculadora
El meu amic no	és gran
El meu tiet no m'	bolígraf
Tinc un	taules

2. Rewrite the sentences in the correct order

a. Em falta fa calculadora una

b. Tinc un vermell regle un llapis i negre

c. La meva molt gran classe és

d. El meu amic llibre blanc té un

e. No blava tinc una agenda

f. A meva tortuga verda tinc una casa

g. El meu és metge pare i a un treballa hospital

3. Spot and correct the grammar and spelling mistakes

a. A meva classe hi ha vint taulas

b. Tenc una calculadora negra

c. Al meu estoig jo té moltes coses

d. El meu amic no tinc res al seu estoig

e. Mi fa falta un llapis i una goma

f. Meu amic Ferran té bolígrafs de tots els color

g. La meva mare és mecànic i treballa a una garatge

h. Soc alt i fort. Tinc els cabells ros i els ulls blau

4. Anagrams

a. toiges

b. pirrassa

c. borlífga

d. teslau

e. relotador

f. quinetama

g. orafesspro

6. Describe this person in the third person (he)

Name: Diego

Pet: A black horse

Hair: brown + blue eyes

School equipment: has pen, pencil, ruler, eraser

Does not have: sharpener, paper, chair

Favourite colour: blue

5. Guided writing: write 3 short paragraphs in the first person singular (I) describing the people below

Person	Lives	Has	Hasn't	Needs
Natalia	Auckland	Exercise book	Pen	Planner
Iker	Pamplona	Ruler	Pencil	Paper
Julieta	Agramunt	Book	Dictionary	Calculator

Tinc *I have*	**No tinc** *I don't have*
Tens *you have*	**No tens** *you don't have*
Té *he/she has*	**No té** *he/she doesn't have*
Tenim *we have*	**No tenim** *we don't have*
Teniu *you guys have*	**No teniu** *you guys don't have*
Tenen *they have*	**No tenen** *they don'thave*

un bolígraf	dotze anys
una calculadora	tretze anys
un quadern	catorze anys
un diccionari	quinze anys
un estoig	setze anys
un llapis	disset anys
un llibre	divuit anys
un ordinador	dinou anys
un retolador	vint anys

classe d'art a les vuit	un ànec
classe de ciència a les nou	un cavall
classe d'espanyol a les deu	un conill
classe de francès a les onze	un gat
classe de geografia a les dotze	un gos
classe d'història a la una	un hàmster
classe de matemàtiques a les dues	un lloro
classe d'educació física a les tres	un ocell
professors molt bons	un peix
professors molt dolents	un ratolí

un fill, una filla	
un germà, una germana	dos avis, dues àvies
un tiet, una tieta	dos cosins, dues cosines dos germans,
un xicot, una xicota *a boyfriend, a girlfriend*	dues germanes

Present indicative of *tenir* + Agreements: Verb drills (1)

1. Match

Tinc	We have
Tenim	I have
Tens	They have
Té	You have
Teniu	He/she has
Tenen	You guys have

2. Complete with the missing word

a. No ___________________ mascotes — *I don't have pets*

b. ___________________ un gat gris — *We have a grey cat*

c. ___________________ dues tortugues — *They have two turtles*

d. ___________________germans? — *Do you have siblings?*

e. ___________________ mascotes? — *Do you guys have pets?*

f. El meu germà ___________ un gos — *My brother has a dog*

g. El meu cosí no _________ mascotes — *My cousin doesn't have pets*

h. Els meus cosins no _________ mascotes — *My cousins have no pets*

3. Complete with the present indicative form of *tenir*

jo   ___________________

tu   ___________________

ell, ella   ___________________

nosaltres   ___________________

vosaltres   ___________________

ells, elles   ___________________

4. Add in the correct verb ending

a. El meu cosí no t____ mascotes

b. Els meus tiets ten______ dos gossos

c. Ara (jo) ti_____ classe d'història

d. A les dotze (nosaltres) ten______ geografia

e. El meu germà t_____ deu anys

f. Els meus pares te_____ quaranta anys

g. El meu pare t____ els cabells blancs

h. Les meves germanes te______ els cabells castanys

5. Complete with the missing form of *tenir*

a. El meu pare ______________ quaranta anys

b. La meva mare ______________ trenta–dos anys

c. Els meus pares ______________ els ulls blaus,
   però jo ______________ els ulls negres

d. El meu tiet Mario no ______________ cabells

e. (tu) ______________ germans?

f. (vosaltres) ______________ els cabells molt bonics

g. (jo) No ______________ mascotes, però el meu
   germà ______________ un conillet d'Índies

6. Translate into Catalan

a. My father has blue eyes

b. I don't have pets

c. I don't have a pen

d. In my pencil case I have a ruler

e. Do you have any felt-tip pens?

f. I have a dog at home

g. My mother is 40

h. My father is 38

i. Do you guys have history today?

j. How old are you?

Present indicative of *tenir* + Agreements
Verb drills (2)

7. Translate the pronoun and verb into Catalan, as shown in the example

a. I have: **Jo tinc**

b. You have:

c. She has:

d. He has:

e. We have:

f. You guys have:

g. They (f) have:

h. They (m) have:

8. Translate into Catalan. Topic: pets and colours

a. We have a blue parrot

b. I have two green turtles

c. My brother has a white rabbit

d. My uncles have a black horse

e. My sister has a red and black spider

f. We don't have pets at home

g. Do you have pets at home?

9. Translate into Catalan. Topic: family members

a. I don't have brothers

b. We have two grandparents

c. My mother has no sisters

d. Do you have any brothers or sisters?

e. Do you guys have cousins?

f. I don't have any brothers

10. Translate into Catalan. Topic: age

a. They are fifteen years old

b. We are fourteen years old

c. I am sixteen years old

d. You guys are twelve years old

e. How old are you?

f. My mother is forty

11. Translate into Catalan. Topic: hair and eyes

a. I have black hair

b. We have blue eyes

c. She has curly hair

d. My mother has blond hair

e. Do you have grey eyes?

f. They have green eyes

g. My brother has brown eyes

h. We have no hair

j. You guys have beautiful eyes

k. My parents have long hair

l. You have no hair

m. My sister has very long hair

Grammar Time 7: Agreements (Part 1)

1. Complete the table

English	Catalan
Yellow	
	Rosa
	Gris
Green	
Red	
	Morat
	Taronja
Black	
	Blanc
Blue	

3. Provide the feminine of each adjective in the table

Masculine	Feminine
groc	
verd	
blau	
vermell	
blanc	
negre	
taronja	

2. Translate into English

a. Un llapis groc ___________________

b. Un estoig negre ___________________

c. Dos quaderns rosa ___________________

d. Tres retoladors vermells ___________________

e. Un regle blau ___________________

f. Dues agendes blaves ___________________

g. Una motxilla taronja ___________________

h. Una maquineta grisa ___________________

i. Un llibre vermell ___________________

j. Una motxilla groga i vermella ___________________

4. Complete with the missing adjective

a. Tinc una motxilla __________ *I have a red schoolbag*

b. Tinc un bolígraf __________ *I have a black pen*

c. Tinc un llibre ____________ *I have a blue book*

d. Tinc un regle ____________ *I have a yellow ruler*

e. Tinc un full ____________ *I have a white sheet of paper*

f. Tinc dues estisores ________ *I have two red scissors*

g. Tinc retoladors ____________ *I have some blue markers*

h. Tinc una motxilla ___________ *I have a black schoolbag*

5. Translate into Catalan

a. a red pen

b. a black ruler

c. a green schoolbag

d. a yellow pencil case

e. two green rulers

f. two blue scissors

g. two pink exercise books

6. Translate into Catalan

a. I have a red pen and a blue pencil

b. He has a green schoolbag

c. Do you have a white pencil case?

d. Do you guys have any red markers?

e. I have a pink sheet of paper

f. We have a yellow schoolbag

g. He has a black and white ruler

UNIT 11
Talking about food, Part 1:
Likes / Dislikes / Reasons

Grammar Time: Menjar / Beure

In this unit you will learn how to say:

- What food you like/dislike and to what extent
- Why you like/dislike it (old and new expressions)
- New adjectives
- The full conjugation of 'menjar' *to eat* and 'beure' *to drink*

You will revisit the following
- Time markers
- Providing a justification

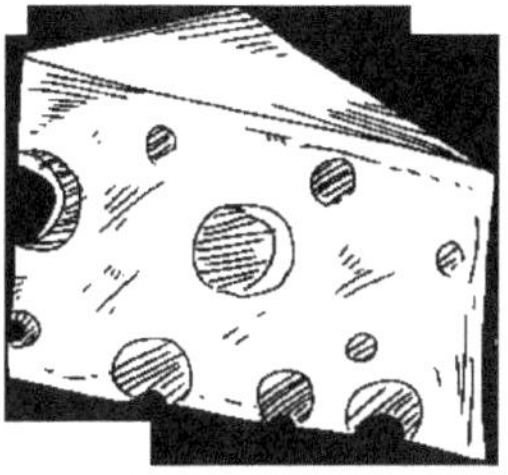

UNIT 11: Talking about food, Part 1
Likes/ Dislikes / Reasons

Singular

M'agrada *I like* **M'agrada molt** *I like a lot* **M'agrada una mica** *I like a bit* **No m'agrada** *I don't like*	**l'arròs** *rice* **el cafè** *coffee* **el formatge** *cheese* **el pa** *bread* **el peix** *fish* **el pollastre a l'ast** *roast chicken* **el suc de fruita** *fruit juice* **la xocolata** *chocolate*	**perquè és** *because it is*	**deliciós** *delicious* **dolç** *sweet* **dur** *tough* **fastigós** *disgusting* **greixós** *greasy* **picant** *spicy* **ric en proteïnes** *rich in protein* **saludable** *healthy*
M'encanta *I love* **Odio** *I hate* **Prefereixo** *I prefer*	**l'aigua** *water* **l'amanida** *the salad* **la carn** *meat* **la fruita** *fruit* **la llet** *milk* **la mel** *honey*	**perquè no és** *because it's not*	**dolça** *sweet* **picant** *spicy* **refrescant** *refreshing* **rica en proteïnes** *rich in protein* **saludable** *healthy*

Plural

M'agraden *I like* **M'agraden molt** *I like a lot* **M'agraden una mica** *I like a bit*	**els ous** *eggs* **els plàtans** *bananas* **els tomàquets** *tomatoes*	**perquè són** *because they are*	**deliciosos** *delicious* **dolços** *sweet* **durs** *tough* **fastigosos** *disgusting*
No m'agraden *I don't like* **M'encanten** *I love* **Odio** *I hate* **Prefereixo** *I prefer*	**les gambes** *prawns* **les hamburgueses** *burgers* **les maduixes** *strawberries* **les pomes** *apples* **les taronges** *oranges* **les verdures** *vegetables*	**perquè no són** *because they are not*	**delicioses** *delicious* **dolces** *sweet* **greixoses** *oily, greasy* **refrescants** *refreshing* **saludables** *healthy*

Unit 11. Talking about food (Part 1): VOCABULARY BUILDING (Part 1)

1. Match

Els plàtans	Eggs
Les maduixes	Apples
La carn	Prawns
El pollastre	Milk
L'aigua	Fruit
La llet	Water
Els ous	Burgers
Les gambes	Chicken
Les hamburgueses	Meat
La fruita	Bananas
Les pomes	Strawberries

2. Complete

a. M'agrada molt el ___________   *I like chicken a lot*

b. M'encanten les ____________   *I love prawns*

c. M'agraden les _____________   *I like strawberries*

d. Prefereixo la ______________   *I love milk*

e. M'encanten els ____________   *I love bananas*

f. M'encanta l' _______ mineral   *I love mineral water*

g. No m'agraden els __________   *I don't like tomatoes*

h. Odio el __________________   *I hate chicken*

i. M'encanta la _______________   *I love fruit*

j. No m'agraden els ___________   *I don't like eggs*

3. Translate into English

a. M'agrada la fruita

b. Odio els ous

c. M'encanta el pollastre rostit

d. M'agraden les hamburgueses

e. Odio la carn

f. Prefereixo les taronges

g. No m'agraden els tomàquets

h. Odio la llet

4. Complete the words

a. Els o________

b. Els pl_____________

c. La fr_______________

d. Les verd___________

e. Les hamb___________

f. Les ga_____________

g. Les po_____________

h. L'a________________

5. Fill the gaps with either *m'agrada* or *no m'agrada*, as per your own preference

a. ____________________el formatge

b. ____________________l'aigua

c. ____________________el pollastre

d. ____________________el cafè

e. ____________________la mel

f. ____________________la carn

g. ____________________la fruita

h. ____________________la llet

i. ____________________el pa

6. Translate into Catalan

a. I like eggs

b. I love oranges

c. I hate tomatoes

d. I don't like prawns

e. I love fruit

f. I don't like vegetables

g. I hate milk

Unit 11. Talking about food (Part 1): VOCABULARY BUILDING (Part 2)

1. Complete with the missing words

a. Aquests plàtans són f________________

These bananas are disgusting

b. Aquestes pomes són d________________

These apples are delicious

c. Aquest pollastre és molt p____________

This chicken is very spicy

d. No m'agrada la c____________________

I don't like meat

e. Aquest cafè és molt d________________

This coffee is very sweet

f. Les hamburgueses no són s____________

Burgers are not healthy

g. Les verdures són s__________________

Vegetables are healthy

h. M'encanta la l____________   *I love milk*

2. Complete the table

Catalan	English
La llet	
	Roast chicken
El peix	
Els ous	
	Water
	Bread
Els cereals	
El pa torrat	
	Vegetables

3. Complete with *m'agrada* or *m'agraden* as appropriate

a. ________________ les pomes

b. ________________ la llet

c. No ________________ els cereals

d. ________________ el pa torrat

e. ________________ les verdures

f. No ________________ la pasta

g. ________________ l'arròs

h. No ________________ el cafè

4. Broken words

a. N__ m' __________ e____ o________   *I don't like eggs*

b. M'e____________ l____ p____________   *I love apples*

c. O______ l___ h________________   *I hate burgers*

d. M'__________ m______ l___ x__________
    I like chocolate a lot

e. E__ c________ e___ d__________   *Coffee is delicious*

f. E__ p______ e__ s__________   *Fish is healthy*

g. E__ curri indi e__ p__________   *Indian curry is spicy*

5. Complete each sentence in a way which is logical and grammatically correct

a. Les ________ no són saludables.

b. Els plàtans són ____________.

c. No m'________ la llet.

d. M'________ el pollastre rostit.

e. ____________ el peix.

f. ____________ la carn vermella
perquè no és saludable.

g. ____________ les verdures
perquè són saludables i delicioses.

Unit 11. Talking about food (Part 1): READING

Hola! Em dic Oriol. Què prefereixo menjar? M'encanta el marisc, llavors m'agraden les gambes i els calamars perquè són deliciosos. També m'agrada molt el peix perquè està molt bo i és ric en proteïnes. Sobretot el salmó.
M'agrada molt el pollastre rostit. A més, m'agrada bastant la fruita, sobretot els plàtans i les maduixes. No m'agraden gaire les verdures perquè no tenen bon gust.
Oriol. 15 anys, Olot

Hola! Em dic Àlex. Què prefereixo menjar? M'encanten les verdures. En menjo cada dia. Les meves verdures preferides són els espinacs, les pastanagues i les albergínies, perquè són riques en vitamines i minerals. També m'agrada la fruita perquè és saludable i deliciosa. Odio la carn i el peix. Són rics en proteïnes però no tenen bon gust.
Àlex. 12 anys, Sitges

Hola! Em dic Violeta. Què prefereixo menjar? M'encanta la carn, sobretot la carn de corder, perquè té molt bon gust. M'agrada molt el pollastre rostit picant perquè té molt bon gust i és ric en proteïnes. M'agraden bastant els ous, Són rics en vitamines i proteïnes. M'agrada bastant la fruita, sobretot les cireres. Són molt bones i són riques en vitamines. No m'agraden gens les pomes. **Violeta. 14 anys, Castelló**

Hola! Em dic Xavier. Què prefereixo menjar? Prefereixo la carn. M'encanta perquè és deliciosa. M'agraden molt les hamburgueses perquè són delicioses. També m'agrada molt la fruita perquè és dolça. No m'agraden les verdures. Odio els tomàquets i les pastanagues. Odio els ous. Són rics en proteïnes i vitamines, però són fastigosos. No m'agraden les patates fregides perquè no són saludables.
Xavier. 9 anys, Tortosa

Hola! Em dic Andreu. Què prefereixo menjar? M'encanta la carn vermella perquè és molt bona i és rica en proteïnes. No menjo gaire peix perquè no m'agrada. M'agraden bastant els calamars fregits, però no són saludables. M'agrada moltíssim la fruita, sobretot els plàtans, perquè són deliciosos, rics en vitamines i no són cars. No m'agraden les pomes i odio les taronges. No menjo verdures. **Andreu. 13 anys, Salou**

1. Find the Catalan in Oriol's text

a. I love seafood

b. I like prawns

c. Are delicious

d. I like fish a lot

e. Salmon

f. I quite like

g. Moreover

h. Above all

i. They are not tasty

2. Andreu o Oriol? Write A or O next to each statement

a. I love seafood - *Oriol*

b. I hate oranges

c. I like fruit a lot

d. I don't like vegetables

e. I prefer salmon

f. I quite like squid

g. I prefer bananas

h. I don't eat much fish

i. I love red meat

3. Complete the statements bellow based on Àlex's text

a. Àlex loves_____________________

b. He eats them _____________________

c. His favourite vegetables are _____________________
_____________________and _____________________

d. He also likes _____________________because it is
_____________________and _____________________

e. He hates _____________________and _____________________

4. Fill in the table below (in English) about Xavier

Loves	Likes a lot	Doesn't like	Hates

Unit 11. Talking about food (Part 1): TRANSLATION

1. Faulty translation: spot and correct (in the English) the translation mistakes

a. M'encanten les gambes: *I hate prawns*

b. Odio el pollastre : *I like meat*

c. M'agrada la mel: *I don't like honey*

d. M'encanten les taronges: *I love apples*

e. Els ous són fastigosos: *eggs are tasty*

f. Els plàtans són rics en vitamines: *bananas are rich in protein*

g. El peix és molt sa: *fish is unhealthy*

h. Prefereixo l'aigua mineral: *I prefer tap water*

i. Odio les verdures: *I love vegetables*

j. M'encanta l'arròs: *I love rice pudding*

k. No m'agrada la fruita: *I quite like fruit*

l. Els calamars fregits són dolços: *fried squid is salty*

2. Translate into English

a. Les gambes són delicioses:

b. El peix és deliciós:

c. El pollastre és ric en proteïnes:

d. M'encanta l'arròs:

e. La carn vermella no és saludable:

f. Uns calamars fregits:

g. Els ous són fastigosos:

h. Prefereixo l'aigua amb gas:

i. M'agraden bastant les gambes:

j. No m'agraden les verdures:

k. M'agraden les pastanagues:

l. Aquest cafè és molt dolç:

m. Una poma fastigosa:

n. Unes taronges delicioses:

3. Phrase-level translation: Eng. to Cat.

a. Spicy chicken:

b. This coffee:

c. I quite like:

d. Very sweet:

e. A disgusting apple:

f. Some delicious oranges:

g. I don't like:

h. I love:

i. Delicious fish:

j. Mineral water:

k. Roast meat:

4. Sentence-level translation: Eng. to Cat.

a. I like spicy chicken a lot

b. I like oranges because they are healthy

c. Meat is tasty but unhealthy

d. This coffee is very sweet

e. Eggs are disgusting

f. I love oranges. They are delicious and rich in vitamins

g. I love fish. It is delicious and rich in protein

h. Vegetables are disgusting

i. I prefer bananas

j. This tea is sweet

Unit 11. Talking about food (Part 1): WRITING

1. Split sentences

M'agrada el pollastre	fruita
Odio les verdures perquè	rostit
Prefereixo la	cafè és dolç
Aquest	són fastigoses
M'agrada bastant la	deliciosos però no són saludables
Els calamars fregits són	els plàtans
M'encanten	carn

2. Rewrite the sentences in the correct order

a. el M' a l'ast pollastre encanta
M'encanta el pollastre a l'ast

b. les verdures Odio

c. cafè Aquest dolç és

d. fregits Els saludables no són calamars

e. l' mineral Prefereixo aigua

f. fastigoses són verdures Les

g. molt les agraden taronges M' són perquè delicioses

3. Spot and correct the grammar and spelling mistakes

a. M'agrada les taronges

b. No agraden les verdures

c. Els ous són fastigoses

d. M'encanta este cafè

e. Prefero les pastanagues

f. Odio la carne

4. Anagrams

a. esFasgosti

b. erudVesr

c. rnCa

d. exiP

e. daSaluble

f. loçD

g. teLl

5. Guided writing: write 3 short paragraphs in the first person singular (I) describing the people below

Person	Loves	Quite likes	Doesn't like	Hates
Natàlia	Chorizo because spicy	Milk because healthy	Red meat	Eggs because disgusting
Iker	Chicken because healthy	Oranges because sweet	Fish	Meat because unhealthy
Júlia	Honey because sweet	Fish because tasty	Fruit	Vegetables because boring

6. Describe this person in the third person (he)

Name: Rafa
Age: 18
Description: Tall, good-looking, sporty, nice
Occupation: Student
Food he loves: Chicken
Food he likes: Vegetables
Food he doesn't like: Red meat
Food he hates: Fish

Grammar Time 8: MENJAR/BEURE
Talking about food, Part 1

Beure *to drink*		
Bec	**aigua** *water*	
Beus	**cafè** *coffee*	
	xocolata desfeta *hot chocolate*	
Beu	**llet** *milk*	
Bevem	**taronjada** *orangeade*	
	te *tea*	
Beveu	**suc de fruita** *fruit juice*	**sovint** *often*
Beuen	**suc de poma** *apple juice*	
Menjar *to eat*		**a vegades** *sometimes*
	arròs *rice*	
	carn *meat*	
	xocolate/a *chocolate*	**de tant en tant**
Menjo	**amanida verda** *green salad*	*from time to time*
	fruita *fruit*	
Menges	**mel** *honey*	**mai** *never*
	pa *bread*	
Menja	**peix** *fish*	
	pollastre a l'ast *roast chicken*	**poques vegades** *rarely*
	formatge *cheese*	
Mengem		**tots els dies** *every day*
	gambes *prawns*	
Mengeu	**hamburgueses** *burgers*	
	ous *eggs*	
	pomes *apples*	
Mengen	**taronges** *oranges*	
	plàtans *bananas*	
	tomàquets *tomatoes*	
	verdures *vegetables*	

1. Match

Menjo	They eat
Menges	He/she eats
Menja	We eat
Mengem	You guys eat
Mengeu	You eat
Mengen	I eat

2. Translate into English

a. Menjo pasta

b. Beu suc de pera

c. Mai menjo carn

d. Menja molt peix

e. Bevem aigua

f. Mai mengen pollastre

g. Sovint menjo arròs

h. Menges pollastre?

i. Què mengeu?

3. Spot and correct the mistakes

a. El meu pare menjo pasta

b. El meu germà i jo no mengem verduras

c. La meva mare mai menga xocolata

d. Els meus germans beveu molt suc de fruita

e. (Jo) Mai beu cafè

f. La meva germana menges carn tots els dies

g. (Vosaltres) Mengen carn de cavall?

h. Què beveu tu?

4. Complete

a. El meu pare __________ molta fruita

b. (Jo) Mai __________ suc de kiwi

c. (Tu) __________ pollastre?

d. La meva mare i jo ______________ molta pasta

e. Els meus pares __________ molta aigua

f. La meva germana __________ molta xocolata desfeta

g. La meva xicota mai ________________ vi

h. (Vosaltres) Què __________________ per esmorzar?

5. Translate into Catalan

a. I eat pasta

b. We drink orange juice

c. What do you eat?

d. What do you guys drink?

e. We eat a lot meat

f. They don't eat a lot of fish

g. She never eats vegetables

h. We drink lots of mineral water

6. Translate into Catalan

a. I never eat red meat. I don't like it because it is unhealthy.

b. I rarely eat sausages. I don't like them because they are oily.

c. I drink fruit juice often. I love it because it is delicious and healthy.

d. I eat paella every day. I love it because it is very tasty.

e. I rarely eat vegetables. They are tasty but I don't like them because they are disgusting.

f. I never drink tea or coffee because I don't like them.

UNIT 12
Talking about food Part 2:
Likes/ Dislikes / Reasons

Grammar Time: Agreement (food)

In this unit you will consolidate all that you learnt in the previous unit and learn how to say:
- What meals you eat every day and
- What you eat at each meal
- The full present indicative conjugation of 'prendre', 'esmorzar', 'dinar' i 'sopar'
- 'This' and 'these' in Catalan

You will revisit the following:
- The full present indicative conjugation of regular AR verbs
- Noun-to-adjective agreement

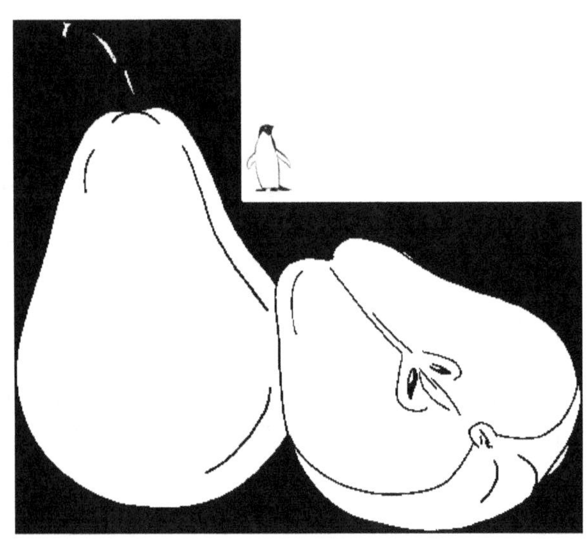

Unit 12
Talking about food Part 2: Likes/ Dislikes / Reasons

Esmorzo *At breakfast I eat* **Dino** *At lunch I eat* **Bereno** *At tea time I eat* **Sopo** *At dinner I eat* **Bec** *I drink*	**arròs** *rice* **cafè** *coffee* **formatge** *cheese* **peix** *fish* **pollastre rostit** *roast chicken* **salmó** *salmon* **suc de fruita** *fruit juice* **tonyina** *tuna fish*	**perquè és** *because it is*	**amarg** *bitter* **deliciós** *delicious* **dolç** *sweet* **fastigós** *disgusting* **greixós** *greasy* **insípid** *bland* **lleuger** *light* **picant** *spicy*
	aigua *water* **amanida verda** *green salad* **carn** *meat* **fruita** *fruit* **llet** *milk* **mel** *honey* **paella** *paella* **xocolata** *chocolate*	**perquè no és** *because it is not*	**gustosa** *tasty* **refrescant** *refreshing* **rica en vitamines** *rich in vitamins* **saludable** *healthy* **sucosa** *juicy*
## Likes/dislikes **M'agraden** *I like* **M'agraden una mica** *I like a bit* **M'agraden molt** *I like a lot* **No m'agraden** *I don't like* **M'encanten** *I love* **Odio** *I hate*	**els calamars** *squid* **els entrepans de formatge** *cheese sandwiches* **els plàtans** *bananas* **els préssecs** *peaches* **els tomàquets** *tomatoes*	**perquè són** *because they are*	**amargs** *bitter* **deliciosos** *delicious* **fastigosos** *disgusting* **rics en vitamines** *rich in vitamins*
	les gambes *prawns* **les hamburgueses** *burgers* **les pomes** *apples* **les salsitxes** *sausages* **les taronges** *oranges* **les verdures** *vegetables*	**perquè no són** *because they are not*	**dolces** *sweet* **greixoses** *greasy* **gustoses** *tasty* **refrescants** *refreshing* **salades** *salty* **saludables** *healthy*

Unit 12. Talking about food – Likes/Dislikes (Part 2): VOCABULARY

1. Match

L'aigua	sandwich
El peix	water
L'arròs	chicken
L'entrepà	fish
El pollastre	cheese
La carn	honey
Els calamars	prawns
Les gambes	strawberries
La mel	sausages
El formatge	rice
Les salsitxes	fruit
Les maduixes	squid
Les verdures	vegetables
La fruita	meat

2. Complete with the missing words

a. M'agrada el _____________   *I like seafood*

b. M'encanta l' _____________   *I love salad*

c. M'agraden molt les __________   *I like vegetables*

d. M'agraden les _____________   *I like apples*

e. Aquest _________ és deliciós   *This chicken is delicious*

f. Aquesta _________ és molt sucosa   *This meat is very juicy*

g. M'agraden molt els __________   *I like bananas a lot*

h. M'encanta la _________   *I love honey*

i. No m'agrada el _____________   *I don't like fish*

3. Complete with the missing letters

a. L'a_ _ _ _ *water*

b. La _ _ _ _ n *meat*

c. La fr_ _ _ _ _ *fruit*

d. La l _ _ _ _ _ _a *lemon*

e. La po_ _ *apple*

f. La pat_ _ _ *potato*

g. El mar_ _ _ _ *seafood*

h. La madu_ _ _ *strawberry*

i. Suc_ _ *juicy*

j. El p_ _ _ _ *fish*

k. Do_ _ *sweet*

l. L'ar_ _ _ _ *rice*

m. El ge_ _ _ _ *ice cream*

n. El pr_ _ _ _ _ _ *peach*

o. La cir_ _ _ _ *cherry*

p. B _ *good*

q. El p_ *bread*

r. Pi_ _ _ _ _ *spicy*

4. Match

Fort	Good
Fregit	Delicious
Dolent	Healthy
Salat	Strong
Saludable	Bad
Bo	Disgusting
Deliciós	Fried
Greixós	Sweet
Fastigós	Greasy
Dolç	Bitter
Amarg	Salty

5. Categories: sort the items below into the appropriate category

a. deliciós	e. bo	i. poma	m. amarg	q. salmó	u. llet
b. dolç	f. gambes	j. maduixa	n. carn	r. pollastre	v. préssecs
c. ric	g. greixós	k. fastigós	o. tonyina	s. dolç	w. pastanagues
d. sucós	h. salat	l. plàtans	p. saludable	t. espinacs	x. formatge

Fruita	Verdura	Adjectius	Peix i carn	Productes lactis

Unit 12. Talking about food – Likes/Dislikes (Part 2): READING

Em dic Robert. Què menjo? Normalment no esmorzo molt. Només una poma o un plàtan i una mica de cafè. No m'agrada el cafè dolç.

Al migdia, en general, dino una hamburguesa amb patates fregides i bec aigua o suc de fruita. Les hamburgueses no són saludables, però em flipen. M'encanta el suc de maduixa. Després de l'escola bereno dues torrades amb mantega i melmelada i bec una tassa de te.

Per sopar menjo força. En general menjo arròs, marisc o pollastre amb verdures i per postres un o dos pastissos. M'agradaria menjar formatge, perquè és deliciós, però la meva mare diu que no és saludable. Ella odia el formatge.

Robert. 12 anys, Palma

Em dic Ferran. Què menjo? Normalment no esmorzo molt. Només ou i una tassa de te. El te m'agrada dolç, amb molt de sucre. A vegades bec suc de pinya.

Al migdia dino pollastre rostit amb verdures i bec aigua mineral. Menjo moltes verdures perquè són molt saludables. M'agradaria menjar gambes perquè m'encanten

Després de l'escola bereno dues torrades amb mel i bec una tassa de te. M'encanta la mel perquè és molt dolça, deliciosa i és rica en vitamines.

Per sopar menjo força. En general menjo arròs, marisc o peix amb verdures i per postres un o dos pastissos. A vegades menjo pollastre perquè és ric en proteïnes, però no m'agrada molt perquè no és molt bo.

Ferran. 10 anys, Figueres

1. Find the Catalan for the words below in Ferran's text

a. Egg :   o___________

b. Tea: t___________

c. Sweet: d___________

d. Sugar: s___________

e. Noon: m___________

f. Chicken: p___________

g. Roast: r___________

h. After: d___________

i. Cup: t___________

j. Honey: m___________

k. Vegetables: v___________

l. Healthy: s___________

m. Delicious: d___________

n. Dinner: s___________

o. Bad: d___________

p. Pastries: p___________

2. Complete the following sentences based on Ferran's text

a. In general, at breakfast I only eat an _________ and a cup of ___________

b. I like tea ___________ with a lot of ___________

c. At __________, for lunch I eat _______ ________ with ___________ and drink ___________ ___________

d. I eat a lot of vegetables because they are ___________ and delicious

e. As a snack I have two ___________ with _______ and drink a ________ of tea

f. At dinner I usually eat ___________, seafood or ________ with ___________ and for dessert, one or two ___________.

g. Sometimes I eat ___________

3. Find the Catalan for the following in both texts

a. I don't have much for breakfast

b. At noon I eat

c. Roast chicken

d. For dessert

e. One or two pastries

f. I would like to eat

g. A cup of tea

h. After school

i. Rice, seafood or fish

j. Toasts with jam

k. Burgers are not healthy

l. Very sweet

m. An apple or a banana

4. Who says this, Robert, Ferran or both?

a. I would love to eat cheese – *Robert*

b. I love honey

c. I love strawberry juice

d. I don't eat much for breakfast

e. I would like to eat prawns

f. I have toasts with jam and butter

g. I am crazy about burgers

h. Burgers are not healthy

i. At dinner I eat quite a bit

j. I drink mineral water

k. His mother hates cheese

l. Sometimes I drink pineapple juice

Em dic Eugènia.

Què menjo? En general al matí menjo molt; un plàtan, dos o tres ous, torrades amb pernil, un suc de fruita i una tassa de cafè. El cafè m'agrada dolç.

Al migdia, en general, dino només arròs amb pollastre o verdures i bec aigua mineral o suc de taronja. M'encanta el pollastre perquè és saludable i és ric en proteïnes. A vegades menjo espàrrecs perquè són amargs i rics en vitamines.

Després de l'escola bereno dues torrades amb mantega i melmelada i bec una tassa de te.

Per sopar menjo molt. En general menjo pasta, carn amb verdures i per postres gelat o pastissos. M'agradaria menjar xocolata, perquè es deliciosa, però la meva mare diu que no és saludable.

Eugènia. 14 anys, Badalona

5. Answer the following questions on Eugènia's text

a. How much does she eat at breakfast?

b. What does she eat for breakfast? 4 things

c. How does she like coffee?

d. What juice does she drink at lunch?

e. What does she have with rice?

f. Why does she like asparagus?

g. What does she put on toasts in the afternoon?

h. Why doesn't her mother allow her to eat chocolate?

6. Find the following in Eugènia's text

a. a word for dessert, starting with P:

b. a vegetable starting with E:

c. a drink starting with S:

d. a type of cold meat starting with P:

e. a fruit starting with P:

f. a dairy product starting with M:

g. an adjective starting with S:

h. a container starting with T:

i. a verb starting with M:

j. a fruit starting with T:

k. an adjective starting with R:

l. a meal starting with B:

Unit 12. Talking about food – Likes/Dislikes (Part 2): WRITING

1. Split sentences

Sempre menjo pollastre	amb llet
Esmorzo cereals	mantega
Menjo una torrada amb	rostit
M'agrada l'amanida	fruita preferida
La carn vermella és	deliciosa però poc saludable
El curri és	o cafè
El plàtan és la meva	verda
Bec te	molt picant

2. Complete with the correct word

a. M'encanta el ___________, sobretot els calamars.

b. En general, ___________ arròs amb pollastre.

c. Normalment ____________cereals, a la cuina.

d. Sempre menjo __________ rostit amb el meu germà.

e. Sopo peix i una amanida____________.

f. Normalment, bereno un entrepà de __________.

g. M'agrada molt la __________ perquè és molt dolça.

h. El cafè és __________, però m'encanta.

i. No m' ___________ la llet, quin fàstic!

j. La fruita és dolça i ____________.

verda	pollastre	dino	formatge	amarg
mel	marisc	esmorzo	agrada	lleugera

3. Spot and correct the grammar and spelling mistakes
Note: in several cases a word is missing

a. En general, dino una hamburguesa amb fregides

b. Bec aigua o fruita.

c. La carn vermella no és saludables, però m'agraden.

d. M'encantan el suc de taronja.

e. Després de l'escola bereno dues torrada mel

f. Bec una tassa de te llet.

g. M'encanta la mel perquè és deliciós i és ric en vitamina.

h. Per sopar jo menges arròs or peix amb verdures.

i. M'encanten les verdures perquè són saludables.

j. El meu peix preferit és el salmó. És deliciosa!

4. Complete the words

a. D_____________ *lunch*

b. S_____________*dinner*

c. E_____________*breakfast*

d. P_____________*spicy*

e. A_____________*bitter*

f. D_____________*sweet*

g. S_____________*healthy*

6. Sentence-level translation: Eng. to Cat.

a. I love fruit juice because it is sweet and refreshing.

b. I don't like salmon because it is disgusting.

c. At tea time I eat a cheese sandwich.

d. I always drink milk with honey. I like it because it's sweet.

e. I like fish, but chicken is not very good.

5. Guided writing: write 3 short paragraphs in the first person singular (I) describing the people below

Person	Lunch	Location	With	After
Eloy	Chicken and rice	The kitchen	Brother	Go to the beach
Samba	Burger	The dining room	Sister	Read a book
Marta	Salad	The garden	Mother	Listen to music

Grammar Time 9: AR Verbs (Part 2)
ESMORZAR, SOPAR, TOMAR and ESMORZAR

ESMORZAR *to eat for breakfast*	**SOPAR** *to eat for dinner*
Esmorzo	**Sopo**
I have... for breakfast	*I eat...for dinner*
Esmorzes *you...*	**Sopes**
Esmorza *she/he...*	**Sopa**
Esmorzem *we...*	**Sopem**
Esmorzeu *you guys...*	**Sopeu**
Esmorzen *they...*	**Sopen**
PRENDRE *to "have"*	**DINAR** *to eat for lunch*
Prenc *I eat*	**Dino** *I eat...for lunch*
Prens	**Dines**
Pren	**Dina**
Prenem	**Dinem**
Preneu	**Dineu**
Prenen	**Dinen**

aigua
un bistec *a steak*
un cafè
carn
cereals amb llet
fruita
gambes
ous *eggs*
llet
marisc
melmelada
mel *honey*
pa
peix
pollastre
formatge
un plàtan
salsitxes
una torrada
verdures
suc de fruites

Author's note: *Prendre is a really handy verb. In the context of food and drink it means the same as to have: like the English "I have a coffee" or "I have some bread for lunch"*

DRILLS

1. Complete with the missing letters

a. (Jo) Esmorz_ cereals amb llet

b. La meva mare pre_ un café

c. Els meus pares pren_ _ un te

d. El meu pare din_ arròs amb pollastre

e. El meus germans no sop_ _ molt

f. (Jo) Din_ fruita o amanida

g. Què esmorz_ _ tu?

h. Què sope_ ells?

i. Els meus pares no esmorz_ _

j. Al migdia el meu amic Pau din_ carn

k. El meu germà i jo sop_ _ molt poc

l. El meu germà gran esmorz_ tres ous

2. Complete with the missing forms of *esmorzar*

a. (Jo) No _______________ molt. Només prenc un cafè

b. La meva mare només _______________ una fruita

c. Els meus pare només _______________ una torrada amb melmelada.

d. La meva germana _______________ cereals amb llet

e. El meu germà i jo _______________ dues torrades amb mantega

f. Què _______________ tu?

g. I vosaltres, què _______________?

3. Spot and correct the errors with the verbs *prendre*, *esmorzar* and *sopar*

a. (Jo) No pren cafè

b. La meva mare sopes un bistec i verdures

c. El meu germà i jo no esmorzen

d. El meu pare mai prenc alcohol

e. El meu amic Paco mai prenen l'esmorzar

f. La meva xicota i jo preneu un cafè amb llet de la cantina de l'escola.

g. La meva xicota mai sopen carn vermella

4. Translate into English

a. La meva mare mai esmorza

b. La meva germana mai dina un bistec

c. A vegades prenc cafè amb llet

d. En general prenem ous per esmorzar

e. Què dines normalment?

f. Només esmorzo una o dues torrades i una tassa de cafè

g. Per esmorzar els meus germans prenen cereals amb llet

6. Translate into Catalan

a. For breakfast I have two eggs and one sausage. Also, I have a coffee with milk.

b. My friend Pau doesn't eat much for lunch. Only chicken with rice.

c. For dinner we eat a lot. We have a steak or fish with potatoes.

d. At noon I have a cup of coffee in the canteen with my girlfriend.

e. My cousin never has red meat. She only eats fish or chicken.

f. My parents eat a lot for lunch. However, my brother and I eat only a salad.

g. My sisters don't eat much for dinner. Generally, they have soup or vegetables.

5. Translate into Catalan

a. For dinner I eat: S_______________

b. For lunch we eat: D_______________

c. For breakfast she has: E_______________

d. They have: P_______________

e. She has: P_______________

f. For dinner we eat: S_______________

g. For lunch you have: D_______________

h. For breakfast they have: E_______________

Grammar Time 10: AGREEMENTS (Part 2) (Food)

El *The* **Aquest** *This*	formatge marisc *seafood* pa peix pollastre porc *pork* suc de fruita	**és** *is*	bo deliciós dolç fastigós greixós picant salat saludable
La, L' *The* **Aquesta** *This*	amanida carn fruita mel melmelada xocolata	**no és** *is not*	bona deliciosa dolça fastigosa greixosa picant salada saludable
Els *The* **Aquests** *These*	**bombons** *chocolates* **dolços** *sweets* **marisc** *seafood* **pastissos** **plàtans** **refrescos** *fizzy drinks*	**són** *are*	bons deliciosos dolços fastigosos greixosos picants salats saludables
Les *The* **Aquestes** *These*	**maduixes** *strawberries* **gambes** **pomes** **salsitxes** **verdures**	**no són** *are not*	bones delicioses dolces greixoses fastigoses picants salades saludables

1. Choose the correct option as shown in the example

	A	B
El peix és	**saludable**	saludabla
Aquest pa és	deliciós	deliciosa
Aquesta carn és	dur	dura
La llet és	fastigosa	fastigós
El porc és	greixós	greixosa
Aquesta poma és	fastigós	fastigosa
Aquesta maduixa és	dolç	dolça
Els mariscs són	saludables	saludablas

2. Complete the table

Masculí	Femení
	fastigosa
deliciós	
	greixosa
dolç	
picant	
	saludable
dolços	
picants	

3. Translate into English

a. Aquestes gambes són fastigoses

b. Aquestes maduixes són delicioses

c. Aquests mariscs són molt gustosos

d. Aquesta poma és repugnant

e. Aquest peix és molt bo

f. Aquest pollastre és massa picant

4. Tick the grammatically correct sentences and correct the incorrect ones

a. Aquestes gambes són molt bones

b. Aquest corder és molt bo

c. Aquest pollastre és molt salats

d. Aquesta poma és molt bona

e. Els mariscs són molt saludable

f. Aquestes salsitxes són molt greixoses

5. Complete

a. El peix és fastigó___

b. Les pomes són saluda___

c. La carn vermella és poc salu___

d. Els pastissos són mass dolç___

e. Els mariscs són molt salu___

f. Aquestes maduixes són delicios___

g. Aquests plàtans són molt delicios___

h. Aquestes gambes són fastigos___

6. Translate into Catalan

a. This fish is disgusting

b. These prawns are delicious

c. This coffee is too sweet

d. These sausages are very fatty

e. These vegetables are very good

f. Oranges are very healthy

g. This paella is very good

Question Skills 2: Jobs/School bag/Food

1. Translate into English

a. On menges al migdia?

b. Quina feina fa la teva mare?

c. Què hi ha a la teva motxilla?

d. Quin és el teu menjar preferit?

e. Quina és la teva beguda preferida?

f. Amb quina freqüència menges carn?

g. T'agrada el suc de fruita?

h. Per què no menges verdures?

i. Menges dolços sovint?

j. Quina feina t'agradaria fer?

k. Com és la teva germana?

l. Amb qui esmorzes normalment?

2. Match the answers below to the questions in activity 1

1. El suc de poma   __e__

2. És intel·ligent i molt graciosa   ______

3. M'agradaria ser jardiner   ______

4. Sí. M'encanta. És deliciós   ______

5. Perquè no m'agraden   ______

6. La paella   ______

7. Sí. Tots els dies   ______

8. Menjo carn dues vegades a la setmana______

9. Hi ha dues llibretes i una agenda   ______

10. La meva mare és policia   ______

11. A la cantina de l'escola   ______

12. Sol   ______

3. Write the questions to the following answers

a. No menjo carn

b. Sempre menjo verdures perquè són saludables

c. Treballo com a bomber

d. M'encanta la fruita perquè és deliciosa i saludable

e. Jugo a futbol a l'escola

f. Sovint menjo marisc

g. Menjo cinc porcions de fruita al dia

h. Soc de Colòmbia

i. No tinc mascotes

j. La meva beguda preferida és el suc de poma

k. El meu pare treballa com a advocat

4. Complete

a. Q_____ h__ __ a __ t__ motxilla?

b. Q_____ f________ fas?

c. Q_____ v____________ menges marisc?

d. Q______ é__ la t___ carn preferida?

e . Q_____ é_ la t__ beguda p_______?

f. P___ q_____ n__ t'ag________ la carn?

g. D__ __ e__ __?

h. A____ q_____ esmorzes normalment?

UNIT 13
Talking about clothes and accessories I wear, how frequently and when

Grammar Time 11: -AR Verbs (Part 2) Portar + Agreements

Revision Quickie 3: Jobs, food, clothes and numbers 20-100

In this unit you will learn how to:

- Say what clothes you wear in various circumstances and places
- Describe various types of weather
- Give a wide range of words for clothing items and accessories
- Use a range of words for places in town
- Make the full present indicative conjugation of *portar* (to wear)

You will revisit:
- Time markers
- Frequency markers
- Colours
- Self-introduction phrases
- Present indicative of *tenir*
- Noun-to-adjective agreement

UNIT 13
Talking about clothes

			blanca *white*
A casa *At home*		una **bufanda** *a scarf*	**blava** *blue*
		una **camisa** *a shirt*	
A la discoteca *At the nightclub*		una **corbata** *a tie*	**grisa** *grey*
		una **faldilla** *a skirt*	**groga** *yellow*
A l'escola *At school*		una **gorra** *a baseball cap*	
		una **jaqueta** *a jacket*	**marró** *brown*
Al gimnàs *At the gym*		una **jaqueta esportiva** *a sports jacket*	**taronja** *orange*
A la platja *At the beach*		una **samarreta** *a T-shirt*	**negra** *black*
		una **samarreta sense mànigues** *tank top*	**verda** *green*
Quan fa calor *When it is hot*	**porto** *I wear*		**vermella** *red*
			blanc *white*
Quan fa fred *When it is cold*		un **abric** *a coat*	**blau** *blue*
		un **banyador** *a swimsuit*	**gris** *grey*
Quan jugo a futbol *When I play football*		un **barret** *a hat*	
		un **cinturó** *a belt*	**groc** *yellow*
Quan surto amb els meus amics / les meves amigues *When I go out with my friends*		un **collaret** *a necklace*	**marró** *brown*
		un **jersei** *a jumper*	**taronja** *orange*
		un **rellotge** *a watch*	
		un **uniforme** *a uniform*	**negre** *black*
Quan surto amb els meus pares *When I go out with my parents*	**porta** *he/she wears*	un **vestit** *a dress / suit*	**verd** *green*
		un **xandall** *a tracksuit*	**vermell** *red*
Quan surto amb el meu xicot/xicota *When I go out with my boyfriend/girlfriend*			
		arracades *(f) earrings*	**blancs / blanques** *white*
		botes *(f) boots*	**blaus / blaves** *blue*
A vegades *Sometimes*		**mitjons** *(m) socks*	**grisos / grises** *grey*
		pantalons *(m) trousers*	**grocs / grogues** *yellow*
Mai *Never*		**pantalons curts** *(m) shorts*	**marrons** *brown*
		sabates *(f) shoes*	**taronja** *orange*
Normalment *Usually*		**sabates de taló** *(f) high heel shoes*	**negres** *black*
Rarament *Rarely*		**sabatilles** *(f) slippers*	**verds / verdes** *green*
		sandàlies *(f) sandals*	**vermelles** *red*
Sempre *Always*		**texans** *(m) jeans*	
		vambes *(f) sports shoes*	

Unit 13. Talking about clothes: VOCABULARY BUILDING

1. Match

Unes arracades	A baseball cap
Una samarreta	Shoes
Un vestit	Trousers
Unes sabates	A suit
Uns pantalons	A T-shirt
Un vestit	Earrings
Una gorra	A dress

2. Translate into English

a. Porto una samarreta negra

b. Porto un vestit gris

c. No porto vambes

d. Porto una gorra blava

e. No porto un rellotge

f. Mai porto arracades

g. Porto un xandall

h. Mai porto vestits

i. Sempre porto sandàlies

j. Mai porto barrets

k. El meu germà sempre porta texans

3. Complete with the missing word

a. A casa _______ una _______________
At home I wear a T-shirt

b. A l'escola porto un _____________ _________
At school I wear a black uniform

c. Al gimnàs ___________ un xandall _________
At the gym I wear a pink tracksuit

d. A la _________ porto un ___________
At the beach I wear a swimsuit

e. ____ ____ discoteca porto un _____________ negre
In the club I wear a black dress

f. Rarament _________ vambes
I rarely wear sports shoes

g. Mai ___________ vestits *I never wear suits*

4. Anagrams: clothes and accessories

a. una rrago

b. un tllogere

c. un titves

d. unes cadesarra

e. unes besatsa

f. una rretasama

g. uns snxate

h. uns jomitns

i. unes batisalles

j. una lladilfa

k. un rertba

l. un retllaco

5. Associations: match each body part below with the words in the box

a. El cap *(head)* – e.g. **gorra**

b. Els peus *(feet)* –

c. Les cames *(legs)* -

d. El coll *(neck)* –

e. El tors *(upper body)* –

f. Les orelles *(ears)* –

g. El canell *(wrist)* –

bufanda	corbata	sabates	botes
jaqueta	camisa	mitjons	**gorra**
arracades	pantalons	faldilla	barret
texans	rellotge	collaret	samarreta

6. Complete

a. Porto bo___________   *I wear boots*

b. A c______________   *At home*

c. Tinc un r__________   *I have a watch*

d. Porto una c_________ vermella
  I wear a red tie

e. Porto un v_________ blau   *I wear a blue suit*

f. El meu germà porta una ja________________
  My brother wears a jacket

g. Ella sempre porta vestits n____________s
  She always wears black dresses

Unit 13. Talking about clothes: READING

Em dic Olivia. Soc de Catalunya. Tinc quinze anys. Soc molt esportista, es per això que tinc molta roba de colors i estils diferents. Prefereixo la roba de bona qualitat però no molt cara. Normalment, a casa porto un xandall. Tinc quatre o cinc xandalls diferents. Quan surto amb la meva xicota porto arracades, un collaret, un vestit vermell o negre i sabates de taló. **Olivia, 15 anys. Catalunya**

En dic Renaud. Soc de França. Tinc tretze anys. M'encanta comprar roba, sobretot sabates. Tinc moltes sabates de marca. M'encanta la roba italiana. Quan fa fred, normalment porto un abric i pantalons negres o morats.
A vegades porto una jaqueta esportiva. Quan fa calor porto samarretes sense mànigues, texans i sandàlies o vambes. A casa meva tinc un cavall que es diu Jacques Chirac. **Renaud, 13 anys. França**

Em dic Gerda. Soc d'Alemanya. Tinc dotze anys. Sempre compro la roba de Zara. M'agrada la roba bonica però no massa cara. No m'agrada la roba de marca. Sempre porto roba esportiva com xandalls, samarretes sense mànigues i vambes. Quan fa fred porto una jaqueta esportiva i xandall. Quan fa calor porto una samarreta i pantalons curts. **Gerda, 12 anys. Alemanya**

Em dic Miguel. Soc d'Argentina. Tinc catorze anys. Quan vaig a l'escola porto una camisa, pantalons i sabates. A casa normalment porto una samarreta i texans. Tinc moltes samarretes i texans a casa. Quan vaig al gimnàs porto una samarreta sense mànigues, pantalons curts i vambes.
Quan vaig al centre comercial amb els meus amics porto una jaqueta, una camisa, uns pantalons negres o grisos i sabates negres. **Miguel, 14 anys. Argentina**

1. Find the Catalan for the following in Olivia's text

a. I am from

b. Sporty

c. Many clothes

d. Good quality clothes

e. A tracksuit

f. When I go out

g. With my girlfriend

h. Earrings

i. A red or black dress

j. High heel shoes

2. Find the Catalan in Miguel's text

a. When I go

b. I wear a shirt

c. T-shirt and jeans

d. At home

e. Tank top

f. With my friends

g. A jacket

h. Black trousers

i. Sports shoes

j. In general

3. Complete the following statements about Renaud

a. He is _________ years old

b. He loves buying _________

c. He has many branded _________

d. When it's cold he wears a _________ __ _________ or _________ _________

e. Sometimes he wears a_________ _________

4. Answer the questions about Gerda (in Catalan)

a. Com es diu?

b. D'on és?

c. Quants anys té?

d. Què li agrada?

e. On compra la roba?

f. Quina roba porta quan fa fred?

g. Quina roba porta quan fa calor?

5. Find someone who

a. ...loves branded clothes

b. ...is from Germany

c. ...wears tank tops in the gym

d. ...wears earrings when she goes out with her girlfriend

e. ...has four or five different tracksuits

f. ...has a lot of T-shirts and jeans at home

g. ...is very sporty

h. ...wears grey or black trousers at the shopping mall

Unit 13. Talking about clothes: WRITING

1. Split sentences

A	samarreta i pantalons curts
Quan fa	casa porto un xandall
Al gimnàs porto una	porto sabates de taló
Quan fa calor porto	fred porto una bufanda
Mai porto	Una samarreta sense mànigues
Quan vaig a la discoteca	texans
Porto pantalons	negra
Porto una samarreta	negres

2. Complete with the correct word

a. __________ surto amb les meves __________ porto roba bonica però còmoda

b. A l'escola __________ un uniforme blau

c. Al gimnàs porto __________

d. A la platja porto un __________

e. Quan __________ calor porto una __________ sense mànigues

f. A casa ____ xandall

g. Quan fa molt fred porto un __________

h. __________ porto botes

abric	amigues	un	porto	quan
vambes	mai	fa	banyador	samarreta

3. Spot and correct the grammar and spelling mistakes
Note: in several cases a word is missing

a. Quan surto meus pares porto un vestit elegant

b. A casa porto una xandall

c. Tinc molta sabates

d. El meu germà sempre porto texans

e. A l'escola un uniforme

f. No m'agrada les robes de marca

g. Quan vaig al centre commercial, normalment porto un jaqueta esportiva

h. Sempre porto vamba

4. Complete the words

a. F__________ *skirt*

b. V__________ *suit*

c. A__________ *earrings*

d. P__________ *trousers*

e. S__________ *shoes*

f. B__________ *scarf*

g. X__________ *tracksuit*

5. Guided writing: write 3 short paragraphs in the first person singular (I) describing the people below

Person	Lives	Always wears	Never wears	Hates
Eulàlia	Lleida	Black dresses	Trousers	Earrings
Arnald	Xàtiva	White T-shirts	Coats	Watches
Jaume	Manacor	Jeans	Shorts	Scarves

6. Describe this person in the third person (he)

Name: Joan

Lives in: London

Age : 20

Pet: A black spider

Hair: Blond

Eyes: Green

Always wears: A suit

Never wears: Jeans

At the gym wears: A tracksuit

Grammar Time 11: AR Verbs (Part 3)
PORTAR + TENIR + AGREEMENTS

PORTAR *to wear*	una **bufanda** *a scarf*	**blava** *blue*
	una **brusa** *a blouse*	**blanca** *white*
Porto *I wear*	una **camisa** *a shirt*	**grisa** *grey*
Portes *you wear*	una **corbata** *a tie*	**groga** *yellow*
Porta *s/he wears*	una **faldilla** *a skirt*	**marró** *brown*
Portem *we wear*	una **gorra** *a baseball cap*	**negra** *black*
Porteu *you guys wear*	una **jaqueta** *a jacket*	**taronja** *orange*
Porten *they wear*	una **samarreta** *a t-shirt*	**verda** *green*
		vermella *red*
TENIR *to have*	un **abric** *a coat*	**blau**
	un **banyador** *a swimsuit*	**blanc**
Tinc *I have*	un **barret** *a hat*	**gris**
Tens *you have*	un **cinturó** *a belt*	**groc**
Té *s/he has*	un **collaret** *a necklace*	**marró**
Tenim *we have*	un **jersei** *a jumper*	**negre**
Teniu *you guys have*	un **rellotge** *a watch*	**taronja**
Tenen *they have*	un **uniforme** *a uniform*	**verd**
	un **vestit** *a suit/a dress*	**vermell**
	un **xandall** *a tracksuit*	

DRILLS

1. Complete with the missing verb endings

a. (jo) Mai port_ faldilles

b. Quina roba port__ tu?

c. El meu germà t___ moltes samarretes

d. Els meus pares port___ roba de marca

e. El meu profe d'art port_ roba molt lletga

f. El meu amic Pau t_ roba molt guai

g. A l'institut *(ells)* port____ uniformes

h. (jo) Ti___molts texans

i. Quina roba port_____? (vosaltres)

j. La meva mare i jo teni_____ molta roba

k. (ell) Mai port_ vestits elegants

l. Quan fa fred, (jo) port_ una bufanda

2. Complete with the missing verbs

a. La meva mare ___________ molta roba de marca

My mother has a lot of branded clothes

b. Els meus germans també __________ samarretes

My brothers also wear T-shirts

c. La meva germana normalment ___________ texans

My sister usually wears jeans

d. Els meus professors sempre ____________ vestits

My teachers always wear suits

e. La meva xicota ___________ moltes arracades

My girlfriend has many earrings

f. Nosaltres _______________ una samarreta negra

We have a black T-shirt

g. Els meus pares__________ molta roba esportiva

My parents wear a lot of sporty clothes

h. Els meus cosins no ____________ molta roba

My cousins don't have many clothes

3. Complete with the correct form of *portar*

a. (jo) Port__ una samarreta

b. La meva mare port__ un vestit elegant

c. Els meus pares no port__ roba de marca

d. Els meus germans port__ texans i samarretes

e. El meu germà i jo port___ roba esportiva

f. La meva germana mai port__ faldilles

g. Quina roba port__ tu?

h. (nosaltres) Mai port_____ gorres

i. Al gimnàs (jo) port___ un xandall

4. Complete with the correct form of *tenir*

a. (jo) No ti___ moltes samarretes

b. Nosaltres no ten_______ roba de marca

c. El meu germà t___ moltes samarretes negres

d. El meu amic Malik no t_______ molta roba
(perquè és un cavall)

e. Els meus germans ten_______ moltes corbates

f. La meva mare t____molts vestits elegants.

5. Translate into English

a. Mai porto samarretes

b. Sempre porta texans

c. No tenim vestits elegants

d. Té moltes sabates

e. Tenen moltes sabates de marca

f. Sempre porten vambes

g. Quina roba portes a l'insitut?

h. Al gimnàs porta un xandall

i. Teniu gorres Adidas?

6. Translate into Catalan

a. Do you have baseball caps?

b. We have many shoes

c. I don't have an elegant dress

d. My father has many suits and ties

e. My mother never wears jeans

f. I never wear trainers

g. What clothes do you wear generally?

h. They never wear uniforms

i. At the gym I wear a tracksuit

j. Do you wear sports clothes often?

Revision Quickie 3: Jobs, food, clothes and numbers 20-100

<table>
<tr><td valign="top">

1. Complete: numbers

a. 100 ce

b. 90 no

c. 30 tr

d. 50 ci

e. 80 vu

f. 60 se

g. 40 qua

</td><td valign="top">

2. Translate into English: food and clothes

a. el vestit   h. el marisc

b. la beguda   i. el peix

c. el pollastre   j. la bufanda

d. la faldilla   k. les sabates

e. el porc   l. les verdures

f. l'aigua   m. el suc

g. la carn   n. el sopar

</td></tr>
</table>

3. Write a word for each letter in the categories below, as shown in the example

Lletra	Roba	Menjar i begudes	Números	Feines
S	samarreta	salsitxa	seixanta	soldat
C				
V				
M				
A				

4. Match

Porto	My name is
Tinc	I drink
Soc	For breakfast i have
Bereno	I live
Menjo	I work
Bec	I have
Esmorzo	For dinner I have
Treballo	There is
Sopo	I am
Visc	For snack i have
Hi ha	I wear
Em dic	I eat

5. Translate into English

a. Mai porto faldilles

b. Sempre bereno torrades amb mel

c. Treballo de dependent

d. Bec cafè sovint

e. No prenc refrescos

f. Sempre esmorzo ous

g. La meva mare és dona de negocis

h. No tinc gaire roba de marca

i. No sopo gaire. Només una amanida

UNIT 14
Saying what I and others do in our free time

Grammar Time: Fer, Jugar, Anar

In this unit you will learn how to say:

- What activities you do using the verbs 'jugar' (play), 'fer' (do) and 'anar' (go)
- Other free time activities

You will revisit:
- Time and frequency markers
- Weather
- Expressing likes/dislikes
- Adjectives
- Pets

UNIT 14
Saying what I (and others) do in our free time

Jugo *I play*	**a bàsquet** *basketball* **a cartes** *cards* **a escacs** *chess* **a futbol** *football* **a tennis** tennis **amb els meus amics** *with my friends*	**a vegades** *sometimes*
Faig *I do*	**ciclisme** *cycling* **els deures** *homework* **equitació** *horse riding* **escalada** *rock climbing* **esport** *sport* **esquí** *skiing* **natació** *swimming* **peses** *weights* **senderisme** *hiking*	**cada dia** *every day* **dues vegades a la setmana** *twice a week* **gairebé mai** *hardly ever* **quan fa bon temps** *when the weather is good*
Vaig *I go*	**a casa del meu amic / la meva amiga** *to my friend's house* **al gimnàs** *to the gym* **a la muntanya** *to the mountain* **al parc** *to the park* **a la piscina** *to the pool* **a la platja** *to the beach* **al poliesportiu** *to the sports centre* **en bici** *on a bike ride* **a córrer** *jogging* **de marxa** *clubbing* **a pescar** *fishing*	**quan fa mal temps** *when the weather is bad* **poques vegades** *rarely* **sovint** *often*

Unit 14. Free time: VOCABULARY BUILDING – Part 1 Weather

1. Match

Jugo a escacs	I go horse-riding
Vaig a córrer	I play chess
Faig equitació	I play basketball
Jugo a cartes	I go hiking
Vaig en bici	I go swimming
Faig natació	I go biking
Faig senderisme	I go jogging
Jugo a bàsquet	I play cards

2. Complete with the missing word

a. Jugo a _______________   *I play chess*

b. _____________ equitació   *I go horse riding*

c. _____________ a cartes *I play cards*

d. Vaig en _______________   *I go cycling*

e. Jugo a _______________   *I play basketball*

f. Vaig a _______________   *I go fishing*

g. Faig _______________   *I go hiking*

h. Faig _______________   *I go rock climbing*

i. Vaig a _______________   *I go jogging*

j. No faig els _____________   *I don't do my homework*

jugo	bàsquet	pescar	escalada	faig
deures	bici	escacs	senderisme	córrer

3. Translate into English

a. Vaig en bici cada dia

b. Faig senderisme sovint

c. Faig escalada dues vegades a la setmana

d. Gairebé mai vaig a natació

e. Quan fa mal temps jugo a cartes o a escacs

f. Jugo a bàsquet sovint

g. Rarament vaig de marxa

h. Vaig a casa del meu amic sovint

i. Vaig a la platja cada dia

j. Vaig a pescar una vegada a la setmana

k. Jugo a golf quan fa bon temps

4. Broken words

a. Faig eq_________________ *I go horse-riding*

b. Faig na_________________*I go swimming*

c. Vaig a pe_________________*I go fishing*

d. Vaig en bi_________________*I go biking*

e. Jugo a es_________________*I play chess*

f. Vaig de ma_________________*I go clubbing*

g. Jugo a ca__________*I play cards*

h. Faig esc_________________*I do rock climbing*

5. *Vaig, jugo* or *faig*?

a. _____________ a bàsquet

b. _____________ en bici

c. _____________ a escacs

d. _____________ a cartes

e. _____________ natació

f. _____________ de marxa

g. _____________ a tennis

h. _____________ peses

i. _____________ escalada

6. Bad translation: spot and fix the translation mistakes

a. Mai vaig de marxa : *I often go clubbing*

b. Jugo a cartes sovint: *I play chess often*

c. Faig escalada poques vegades: *I go swimming rarely*

d. Quan fa bon temps vaig a córrer: *When the weather is nice I go hiking*

e. Vaig en bici dues vegades a la setmana: *I go biking every day*

f. Gairebé mai jugo a escacs: *I never play chess*

g. Faig senderisme sovint: *I never go hiking*

h. Faig natació sovint: *I go swimming from time to time*

Unit 14. Free time: READING

Em dic Thomas Weidner. Soc alemany. En el meu temps lliure faig molt esport. El meu esport preferit és l'escalada. Faig escalada cada dia. Quan fa mal temps em quedo casa *[I stay at home]* i jugo a escacs o a cartes. També m'agrada molt jugar amb videojocs o a la Play. Jugo a la Play sovint.
Thomas, 9 anys. Alemanya

Em dic Verónica Palacín. Soc de Barbastro, a l'Aragó. Soc pèl-roja, molt simpàtica i divertida, però no soc molt esportista. Prefereixo llegir llibres *[read books]*, jugar amb videojocs o a escacs i escoltar música. Quan fa bon temps vaig a córrer al parc del meu barri o jugo a tennis amb el meu germà. No m'agrada anar al gimnàs ni a la piscina. Odio la natació perquè no m'agrada l'aigua.
Verónica, 17 anys. Barbastro

Em dic Olga. Soc de Xipre. En el meu temps lliure m'agrada molt llegir libres i diaris. També m'agrada jugar a cartes i a escacs. No soc molt esportista. Però, a vegades vaig al gimnàs i faig peses. A més a més, al cap de setmana, quan fa bon temps, faig senderisme al camp amb el meu gos. El Buddy és un gos salsitxa i és petit i marró.
Olga, 14 anys. Xipre

Em dic Jérôme. Soc francès. M'encanta anar en bici. Vaig en bici cada dia amb els meus amics. És el meu esport preferit. A vegades faig escalada, senderisme, o vaig a córrer. No m'agrada el tennis ni el futbol. Odio fer natació. Faig natació poques vegades. Dues vegades a la setmana vaig de marxa amb el meu amic, Julien. M'encanta ballar.
Jérôme, 12 anys. França

1. Find the Catalan for the following in Thomas' text

a. I do a lot of sport

b. My favourite sport

c. Climbing

d. Every day

e. When the weather's bad

f. I play chess

g. Also

h. I play on the Playstation

2. Find the Catalan in Jérôme's text for

a. I love biking

b. with my friends

c. sometimes

d. I do swimming

e. I go clubbing

f. I go rock climbing

g. with my friend, Julien

3. Complete the following statements about Verónica

a. She is from _______________

b. She is not very ____________

c. She plays videogames and ____________

d. When the weather is nice she _______________

e. She also plays tennis with her_________________________

f. She doesn't enjoy the gym nor the __________________

4. List 8 details about Olga

1.

2.

3.

4.

5.

6.

7.

8.

5. Find someone who

a. ...enjoys reading newspapers

b. ...hates swimming

c. ...does a lot of sport

d. ...does weight lifting

e. ...goes clubbing twice a week

Unit 14. Free time: TRANSLATION

1. Gapped translation

a. Mai vaig de marxa — *I _______ go clubbing*

b. Jugo a la Play sovint — *I often play _____________*

c. No jugo a tennis gairebé mai — *I _________ _________ play tennis*

d. Jugo a_______________ — *I play chess*

e. Jugo a ____________ — *I play cards*

f. A vegades vaig en bici — *_____________, I go cycling*

g. Mai faig peses — *I never do __________________*

h. Quan fa _________ temps vaig a córrer
   When the weather is nice, I go jogging

2. Translate to English

a. Gairebé mai

b. A vegades

c. Quan fa mal temps

d. A casa del meu amic

e. Mai

f. Cada dia

g. Faig escalada

h. Vaig de marxa

i. Vaig a pescar

3. Translate into English

a. Mai vaig a pescar amb el meu pare

b. Jugo a cartes amb el meu germà

c. Faig senderisme amb la meva mare

d. Jugo a escacs amb la meva millor amiga

e. Gairebé mai jugo a la Play amb el meu cosí

f. Vaig de marxa cada dissabte

4. Translate into Catalan

a. *Bike*: B

b. *Rock climbing*: E

c. *Basketball*: B

d. *Fishing*: P

e. *Weights*: P

f. *Videogames*: V

g. *Chess*: E

h. *Cards*: C

i. *Hiking*: S

j. *Jogging*: C

5. Translate into Catalan

a. I go jogging

b. I play chess

c. I 'do' rock climbing

d. I 'do' swimming

e. I 'do' horse riding

f. I do weights

g. I go clubbing

h. I play videogames

i. I 'do' cycling

j. I 'do' hiking

Unit 14. Free time: WRITING

1. Split sentences

Mai	al parc
Jugo a escacs	esport
Vaig a casa	faig escalada
Vaig a córrer	sovint
Jugo a	bici
Faig molt	del meu amic Ovidi
Vaig en	gimnàs
Faig peses al	cartes

2. Complete the sentences

a. Mai ____________ a córrer

b. A vegades ____________ a escacs

c. ____________ escalada de tant en tant

d. ____________ equitació sovint

e. Jugo a tennis ____________ dia

f. Vaig a ____________ del meu amic

g. En el meu ____________ lliure

h. Faig ____________ al gimnàs

i. Faig ____________ deures

3. Spot and correct the mistakes
Note: in some cases a word is missing

a. Jugo tenis

b. Jugo escacs

c. Vaig a casa del amic

d. Gairebé mai vaig a bici

e. Vaig meus deures

f. Vaig natació

g. Faig pes

4. Complete the words

a. Esc____________

b. Bas____________

c. Sende____________

d. Video____________

e. Equi____________

f. M____________

g. S____________

5. Write a paragraph for each of the people below in the first person singular (I)

Name	Sport I do	How often	Who with	Where	Why I like it
Magalí	Hiking	Every day	With my family	In the countryside	It's fun
Dylan	Weight-lifting	Often	With my friend James	At home	It's healthy
Aleix	Jogging	When the weather is nice	Alone	In the park	It's relaxing

Grammar Time 12: *Jugar, Fer* and *Anar* (Part 1)

Jugar *to play*		
Jugo *I play* **Jugues** *you play* **Juga** *he/she plays* **Juguem** *we play* **Jugueu** *you guys play* **Juguen** *they play*	**a escacs** *chess* **a bàsquet** *basketball* **a cartes** *cards* **a futbol** *football* **a tennis** tennis **amb els meus amics** *with my friends*	**sovint** *often*
Fer *to do*		**a vegades** *sometimes*
Faig *I do* **Fas** **Fa** **Fem** **Feu** **Fan**	**ciclisme** *cycling* **esport** *sport* **equitació** *horse riding* **escalada** *rock climbing* **natació** *swimming* **els deures** *homework* **peses** *weights*	**gairebé mai** *hardly ever* **dues vegades a la setmana** *twice a week*
Anar *to go*		
Vaig *I go* **Vas** **Va** **Anem** **Aneu** **Van**	**a casa del meu amic** *to my friend's (M) house* **a casa de la meva amiga** *to my friend's (F) house* **a la muntanya** *to the mountain* **a la piscina** *to the pool* **a la platja** *to the beach* **al gimnàs** *to the gym* **al parc** *to the park* **de marxa** *clubbing* **a pescar** *fishing* **a córrer** *running* **en bici** *on a bike ride*	**poques vegades** *rarely* **cada dia** *every day*

1. Match

Faig	He/she does
Fas	We do
Fa	You do
Fem	I do
Feu	They do
Fan	You guys do

2. Complete with the correct ending

a. (jo) Mai fa___ els meus deures

b. El meu pare ju___ a futbol sovint

c. Quin esport f__ tu?

d. (nosaltres) Mai jug______ a tennis

e. (vosaltres) Què f____ avui?

f. Les meves germanes sempre jug___ a la Play

g. (jo) Mai ju___ amb videojocs

h. El meu germà gran f___ arts marcials

i. El meus germans no jug___ a escacs

j. La meva mare i jo jug______ a cartes

3. Write the correct form of *jugar* (to play)

a. I play   ______________

b. You play   ______________

c. She plays   ______________

d. We play   ______________

e. You guys play   ______________

f. They play   ______________

g. My brothers play   ______________

h. You and I play   ______________

i. He and I play   ______________

4. Complete with *faig, vaig* or *jugo*

a. Mai ____________ a bàsquet

b. ____________ esport cada dia

c. ____________ a voleibol

d. ____________ a cartes poques vegades

e. Mai ____________ ciclisme

f. ____________ a la Play cada dia

g. ____________ a pescar poques vegades

h. ____________ escalada sovint

i. ____________ a l'estadi amb la meva mare

5. Spot and correct the translation mistakes (in the English)

a. Vaig a pescar   *You go fishing*

b. Vas al cine   *You go to the igloo*

c. Anem al centre comercial
   You guys go to the shopping mall

d. Mai vaig a casa de la Marta
   We never go to Marta's house

e. Van al cine una vegada a la setmana
   She goes to the cinema once a week

6. Complete the forms of *anar* below

a. V_ _ _ a pescar   *I go fishing*

b. V_ _ al parc   *They go to the park*

c. A_ _ _a la platja   *We go to the beach*

d. V_ _ a la piscina   *They go to the swimming pool*

e. On a_ _ _ ?   *Where are you going?*

7. Complete with *fa, juga* or *va*

a. La meva mare mai __________ esport.

b. El meu pare rarament________ a la sinagoga.

c. El meu germà______ a la mesquita cada divendres.

d. El meu avi mai ________ a cartes amb mi.

e. El meu germà gran __________ arts marcials.

f. El meu amic Adrià __________ a la Play.

g. El meu germà petit________ ciclisme sovint.

h. La meva àvia _____ a la platja cada dia.

8. Complete with *fan, juguen* or *van*

a. Els meus pares mai __________ a bàsquet.

b. Els meus germans no __________ esport.

c. Els meus germans mai ______ a futbol.

d. La meva mare i el meu pare ________ a cartes.

e. Els meus cosins ________ arts marcials.

f. Elles ________ a pescar sovint.

g. Els meus tiets __________ a la biblioteca poques vegades.

h. Els meus amics mai __________ escalada amb mi.

i. Els teus amics __________ ciclisme?

j. Els meus amics, Marc i Sara, ______ a escacs.

k. Ells ____________ a la piscina.

9. Translate into English

a. Mai jugo a futbol

b. Fa els seus deures sovint

c. Mai anem a l'església

d. No van sovint a la piscina

e. Quan fa bon temps, van al parc

f. Mai jugo a escacs

g. Quan fa mal temps vaig al gimnàs

10. Translate into Catalan

a. We never go to the swimming pool

b. They do sport rarely

c. She plays basketball every day

d. When the weather is nice, I go jogging

e. I rarely do cycling

f. I do rock climbing often

g. My father and I often play badminton

h. My sister plays tennis twice a week

i. I go to the swimming pool on Saturdays

j. When the weather is bad I go to the gym

k. They rarely do their homework

l. We never play chess

UNIT 15
Talking about weather and free time

GRAMMAR TIME: Jugar / Fer / Anar
Question skills: Clothes / Free time / Weather

In this unit you will learn how to say:
- What free-time activities you do in different types of Weather
- Where you do them **and** who with
- Words for places in town

You will also learn how to ask and answer questions about:
- Clothes
- Free time
- Weather

You will revisit:
- Sports and hobbies
- The verbs 'fer', 'anar' and 'jugar' in the present indicative
- Pets
- Places in town
- Clothes
- Family members
- Numbers from 1 to 100

Unit 15
Talking about weather and free time

<table>
<tr>
<td rowspan="2">

A vegades *Sometimes*

Entre setmana *On weekdays*

Els caps de setmana

At the weekends

Quan tinc temps

When I have time

Quan el cel està clar

When the sky is clear

Quan està ennuvolat

When the sky is cloudy

Quan fa bon temps

When the weather is good

Quan fa mal temps

When the weather is bad

Quan fa calor *When it is hot*

Quan fa fred *When it is cold*

Quan fa sol *When it is sunny*

Quan fa vent *When it is windy*

Quan hi ha boira

When it is foggy

Quan hi ha tempestes

When there are storms

Quan plou *When it rains*

Quan neva *When it snows*

</td>
<td colspan="2">

jugo *I play*

la meva amiga Maria juga
my friend Maria plays

</td>
<td>

a bàsquet *basketball*
a cartes *cards*
a escacs *chess*
a futbol *football*
a tennis *tennis*
amb els meus amics *with my friends*
amb els seus amics *with his/her friends*

</td>
</tr>
<tr>
<td colspan="2">

faig *I do*

el meu amic Francesc fa
my friend Francesc does

</td>
<td>

ciclisme *cycling*
equitació *horse riding*
escalada *rock climbing*
esport *sport*
natació *swimming*
els deures *hw*
senderisme *hiking*

</td>
</tr>
</table>

<table>
<tr>
<td colspan="2">

vaig *I go*

el meu amic va
my friend (m) goes

la meva amiga va
my friend (f) goes

</td>
<td>

a casa del meu amic / de la meva amiga *to my friend's house*
a casa del seu amic / de la seva amiga *to his/her friend's house*

a córrer *jogging*
a esquiar *skiing*
a pescar *fishing*

al camp *to the countryside*
al centre comercial *to the mall*
al gimnàs *to the gym*
a la muntanya *to the mountain*
al parc *to the park*
a la piscina *to the pool*
a la platja *to the beach*
al poliesportiu *to the sports centre*
de marxa *clubbing*
en bici *on a bike ride*

</td>
</tr>
</table>

<table>
<tr>
<td colspan="2">

em quedo *I stay*

</td>
<td>

a casa meva *in my home*
a la meva habitació *in my room*

</td>
</tr>
<tr>
<td>

**l'Antoni
la Tura**

</td>
<td>

es queda *stays*

</td>
<td>

a casa seva *in his/her home*
a la seva habitació *in his/her room*

</td>
</tr>
</table>

Unit 15. Talking about weather and free time VOCABULARY BUILDING 1

1. Match

Quan	It's cold
Fa fred	It's hot
Fa calor	It's clear skies
Fa bon temps	When
Fa mal temps	It's good weather
El cel està clar	It's raining
Plou	It's bad weather

2. Translate into English

a. Quan fa fred

b. Quan plou

c. El cel està clar

d. Quan fa calor

e. Quan neva

f. Quan fa bon temps

g. Quan hi ha boira

h. Jugo a tennis

i. Esquio

j. Quan fa mal temps

3. Complete with the missing word

a. Quan fa __________ temps
   When it's bad weather

b. Quan _________ i fa ________
   When it rains and is cold

c. Quan ________ sol i fa ________
   When it is sunny and hot

d. Quan hi ha tempesta em _________ a casa
   When it is stormy I stay at home

e. Quan fa __________ temps vaig al parc
   When it's good weather I go to the park

f. Quan _________ esquio a la muntanya
   When it snows I ski on the mountain

g. Quan fa mal _________ el meu amic es queda a casa
   When the weather is bad my friend stays at home

h. M'agrada quan fa ______ *I like it when it's sunny*

4. Anagrams: weather

a. fder	e. larc	i. ahih raboi
b. orcal	f. lam sptem	j. lavotennu
c. neav	g. af ols	k. tapestem
d. oupl	h. vten	l. nob pstem

5. Associations: match each weather word below with the clothes/activities in the box

a. Mal temps: tempesta, vent, pluja –

b. Fa bon temps: sol i calor –

c. Neva i fa fred –

Botes de neu	em quedo a casa	esquio	la platja
no faig res	pantalons curts	miro la tele	barret
la muntanya	bufanda	pijama	banyador

6. Complete

a. Fa bon _________ *It's good weather*

b. Em quedo a c______ *I stay at home*

c. Quan p_________ *When it rains*

d. M' __________ quan fa calor
   I like it when it's hot

e. ______ a la platja *I go to the beach*

f. Quan ______ tempestes
   When there are storms

g. Quan el _______ està clar
   When the sky is clear

h. Quan està ____________
   When it is cloudy

Unit 15. Talking about weather and free time: VOCABULARY BUILDING 2

1. Match

Jugo a tennis	I go clubbing
Jugo a cartes	In his bedroom
Faig equitació	She goes fishing
Vaig de marxa	I play tennis
Ella va a pescar	I do horseriding
Al seu dormitori	I play cards
Em quedo a casa	Swimming
La natació	I stay at home

2. Complete with the missing word

a. Em quedo al ____ dormitori   *I stay in my bedroom*

b. El meu amic ____ a la platja   *My friend goes to the beach*

c. Vaig a ______ de la meva ____   *I go to my friend's house*

d. Vaig al ______________   *I go to the sports centre*

e. Sempre faig els deures___________ setmana
    I always do my homework on weekdays

f. M'agraden els caps de __________ *I like the weekends*

g. Jugo amb les meves _________ *I play with my friends*

h. La meva amiga Vero sempre ____ a casa del ___ amic
    My friend Vero always goes to her friend's house

i. Sempre faig _________ *I always do hiking*

3. Translate into English

a. La casa del meu amic

b. Faig equitació

c. El cel està clar

d. Faig escalada

e. Vaig a córrer

f. Vaig al poliesportiu

g. Vaig a la piscina

h. Faig esport

4. Anagrams: activities

a. rrrcóe

b. naciató

c. sendsmerie

d. equtiació

e. bàtsque

f. buftol

g. trecas

h. csesca

i. cernte corcmeial

j. de xamra

k. a pecsar

l. poesrt

5. Broken words

a. J________ a f_______a_____ els meus a_______s
    I play football with my friends

b. La m__________ t_______ M______ j_______ a c_______
    My aunt Maria plays cards

c. V____ a c___ d_ m__ a________
    I go to my friend's house

d. E Q______ v_ a_ p_______________
    Quim goes to the sports centre

e. F____ e___________ a___ el m___ c_______
    I do horse riding with my horse

f. El m__ a_____ e__ q_____ a c____ i fa e___ d______
    My friend stays at home and does homework

6. Complete

a. Faig els _________ *I do homework*

b. Es __________ a casa
    He stays at home

c. Fa _________ *He does swimming*

d. Vaig __ gimnàs *I go to the gym*

e. ______ a la piscina *I go to the pool*

f. Em quedo a _______ *I stay home*

g. Faig _________ *I do climbing*

h. Faig __________ a la _________
    I do hiking in the mountain

i. A la meva ____________ *In my room*

Unit 15. Talking about weather and free time: READING

Em dic Dafydd. Soc de Swansea, a Gal·les. Tinc onze anys. Soc molt esportista, llavors m'agrada quan fa bon temps. Quan fa sol sempre vaig al parc amb els meus amics i jugo a futbol. També, quan fa calor sempre vaig a la platja amb el meu gos. És petit i negre, i molt simpàtic. Porto un banyador, sandàlies i un barret quan vaig a la platja. **Dafyyd, 11. Gal·les**

Em dic Chloé. Soc de França. Tinc catorze anys. Quan fa calor i fa bon temps vaig a la piscina i faig natació. També vaig a pescar amb el meu pare a la seva barca. És una mica avorrit però tot i així m'agrada. A la nit vaig de marxa amb els meus amics. Quan vaig a la discoteca normalment porto una samarreta i uns texans. La meva amiga es diu Sofia. És simpàtica i intel·ligent. Si fa mal temps i plou ella sempre es queda a casa seva i fa els deures. **Chloé, 14 anys. França**

Em dic Claudia. Soc de Roma, a Itàlia. Tinc quinze anys. M'encanta comprar samarretes i jaquetes. M'encanta quan hi ha tempestes. Em quedo a casa amb el meu germà gran i jugo a videojocs o a cartes amb ell. Les tempestes són molt boniques i divertides. No m'agrada quan fa fred perquè no m'agrada portar abrics i bufandes. A casa tinc un gos, un gat i un lloro que parla italià! **Claudia, 15 anys. Itàlia**

1. Find the Catalan for the following in Dafydd's text

a. I am from

b. I am 11

c. I like it

d. when

e. it is sunny

f. I go to the park

g. with my dog

h. small and black

i. a swimsuit

j. the beach

2. Find the Catalan for the following in Chloe's text

a. when it's hot

b. the weather is good

c. I swim

d. I go fishing

e. a bit boring

f. I go clubbing

g. a t-shirt

h. is called

i. stays

j. in her house

Em dic Ares. Soc de Brasil. Tinc dotze anys. M'agrada cantar en el meu temps lliure. Quan fa fred vaig al centre comercial amb les meves amigues. Porto un abric, una bufanda i unes botes. M'encanta el fred! La meva pel·lícula preferida és Frozen 2. Quan fa calor em quedo a casa perquè no m'agrada. Mai vaig a la platja. Odio la platja! **Ares, 12 anys. Brasil**

3. Complete the following statements about Claudia

a. She is _________ years old

b. She loves buying ___________ and ____________

c. She loves it when there are _________

d. When it's stormy she plays _________ or _________ with her _________ brother

e. Claudia does not like _________weather

f. Her pet can ___________ Italian

4. Answer the questions about Ares (in Catalan)

a. D'on és?

b. Quants anys té?

c. Què fa en el seu temps lliure?

d. Quin temps li agrada?

e. On va quan fa fred?

f. Què fa quan fa calor?

g. Li agrada la calor?

h. Quina és la seva pel·lícula preferida?

5. Find someone who

a. ...likes to go fishing
b. ...is from France
c. ...loves really cold weather
d. ...has three pets at home
e. ...thinks that storms are pretty
f. ...wears jeans to go out
g. ...goes to the beach with an animal
h. ...never goes to the beach
i. ...owns a boat

Unit 15. Talking about weather and free time: WRITING

1. Split sentences

M'agrada molt quan	sol vaig a la platja
No m'	un abric i una bufanda
Quan fa	fa fred
Quan fa molt fred porto	agrada la pluja
Les tempestes són	esquio
Quan fa mal temps	em quedo a casa
Quan fa bon	molt boniques
Quan neva	temps vaig al parc

2. Complete with the correct option

a. ___________ fa fred porto una bufanda. No m' ___________!

b. ___________ setmana faig els deures

c. Quan _________ mal temps em _________ a casa

d. Quan _________ boira no vaig a la ____________

e. Quan fa __________ vaig a la platja

f. Quan el cel està _______ faig senderisme al camp

g. Quan fa mal temps el meu amic Pepe es queda a casa _______

calor	hi ha	quedo	muntanya	entre
agrada	fa	quan	clar	seva

3. Spot and correct the grammar and spelling mistakes
   Note: in several cases a word is missing

a. Quan és vent vig al gimnàs amb el meu amic

b. Quan fa ennuvolat la meva amiga Joana jugas a tennis

c. M'encanten les tempesta, són molt bonica

d. Quan fa mal temp meu amic se queda a casa

e. Quan boira no jugo a bàsquet

f. Els caps de semana vaig a la platja meu gos

g. Quan fa sol vaig al camp porta una samarreta blanc

h. (jo) Sempre porta vambes quan a futbol

4. Complete the words

a. F___________ *cold*

b. C___________ *hot*

c. E___________ *cloudy*

d. Q_________ *when*

e. T___________ *storms*

f. V___________ *wind*

g. B__________ *fog*

6. Describe this person in the third person (she)

Name: Paula

Lives in: Maó

Age : 13

Pet: A white dog

Weather: Sunny and good weather

Always: Goes to the countryside and does hiking

Never: Stays at home and does homework

5. Guided writing: write 3 short paragraphs in the first person singular (I) describing the people below

Person	Lives	Weather	Activity	With
Rosa	Sant Feliu de Guíxols	Cold and rainy	Stay at home	Older sister
Paula	Blanes	Hot and sunny	Go to the beach	Dog
Jesús	Huelva	Good weather	Go to the park	His boyfriend

Grammar Time 13: Jugar, Fer, Anar + Ser i Tenir

Jugar – To play		
*(jo) jugo *I play* (tu) jugues *you...* (ell) juga *he...* (ella) juga *she...*	(nosaltres) juguem *we play...* (vosaltres) jugueu *you guys ...* (ells) juguen *they... masc/**mixed* (elles) juguen *they... all female*	a bàsquet a cartes a escacs amb els meus amics/les meves amigues

Fer – To do		
faig fem fas feu fa fan	esport els deures	natació peses *(weights)*

Anar – To go		
vaig anem vas aneu va van	a la piscina a córrer a pescar en bici	al gimnàs al parc

Ser – To be

		Masc. sing	Fem. sing	Masc. plural	Fem. plural
soc som		alt	alta	alts	altes
ets sou		guapo	guapa	guapos	guapes
és són		francès	francesa	francesos	franceses
		alemany	alemanya	alemanys	alemanyes

Tenir – To have		
tinc tenim tens teniu té tenen	dos germans els ulls negres el cabell castany	onze anys un gos i un gat

* **Author's note:** *the subject pronouns* jo, tu, ell, ella, nosaltres, vosaltres, ells, elles *are OPTIONAL, not obligatory. They are useful to:*
  1) *Add emphasis*
  2) *Help know who we are talking about in the third person (he/she)*

** Ells *means "they" and should be used for a group of males AND/OR a mixed group of males and females.*

1. Complete with the one of the following verbs: *Tinc – Vaig – Soc – Jugo – Faig*

a. __________ esport

b. __________ al parc

c. __________ un gat

d. __________ a futbol

e. __________ a cartes

f. __________ un gos

g. __________ quinze anys

h. __________ dues mascotes

i. __________ al cine

j. __________ escalada

k. __________ ciclisme

l. __________ a escacs

m. __________ a bàsquet

n. __________ el ulls negres

o. __________ rossa

2. Rewrite the sentences in the third person singular (he/she)

jo	ell , ella
Jugo a tennis	
vaig al cine	
tinc un gat	
soc alta	
faig natació	

4. Complete

a. Jo mai v__________ a la piscina

b. La meva mare mai v__________ a la perruqueria

c. (nosaltres) A__________ a la platja sovint

d. El meu g__________ té un gat

e. Ells s______ anglesos, jo s______ italià

f. El meus pares t__________ el cabell pèl-roig

g. La meva germana i jo f__________ arts marcials

5. Complete with the appropriate verb

a. (jo) mai ______ al cine amb la meva mare

b. La meva gemana i jo ________ al parc

c. La meva mare __________ quaranta anys

d. El meu cosí ______ molt alt i guapo

e. Els meus germans __________ a la Play sovint

f. (ell) Mai ______ esport

g. Quan fa bon temps (ell) ____ a la platja

3. Translate into English

a. Fem natació

b. Juguem a escacs

c. No fan res

d. Van al cine

e. Tenim dos gossos

f. Som francesos

g. No té germans

h. No soc de Reus

i. No faig res

6. Translate into Catalan

a. I never play tennis with him

b. My mother never goes to church

c. My brother is tall and slim. He has blond hair and blue eyes

d. My father is forty years old

e. My brother goes to the gym every day

f. They never go to the swimming pool

Revision Quickie 4: Clothes/Free time/Weather

1. Activities: Match

Faig els deures	I go to the library
Faig esport	I go to the swimming pool
Jugo a bàsquet	I go to the gym
Jugo a cartes	I go window shopping
Vaig a la biblioteca	I do the homework
Vaig a la piscina	I go swimming
Vaig al gimnàs	I do rock climbing
Miro aparadors	I do sport
Faig natació	I go horse-riding
Faig equitació	I go to the beach
Vaig a la platja	I play cards
Faig escalada	I play basketball

2. Complete: weather

a. Fa fr_ _ _

b. Fa ca_ _ _ _

c. Fa s_ _

d. Hi ha b_ _ _ _ _

e. Fa b_ _ _ t_ _ _ _ _

f. Fa ma_ t_ _ _ _ _

g. Hi ha una t_ _ _ _ _ _ _ _

h. Fa v_ _ _

i. P _ _ _ _

3. Fill in the gaps

a. Quan fa f_______, porto un a____________   *When it is cold I wear a coat*

b. Quan fa m_____ t_________, em q________ a casa   *When the weather is bad I stay at home*

c. Quan f____ s______ vaig a la p_________   *When it is sunny I go to the beach*

d. Quan v_____ al gimnàs, p________ un x___________   *When I go to the gym I wear a tracksuit*

e. Quan fa c_________, vaig a l_ p_____________   *When it is hot I go to the swimming pool*

f. El cap de setmana f______ els m____ d____________ *At the week-end I do my homework*

g. Quan t_________ t_________ ll_________   *When I have free time*

h. F________ e________________   *I go rock climbing*

4. Translate into Catalan

a. When it is hot

b. When it is cold

c. I play basketball

d. I do my homework

e. I go rock climbing

f. When I have free time

g. I go to the swimming-pool

h. I go to the gym

5. Translate to Catalan

a. I wear a coat

b. We wear a uniform

c. They play basketball

d. She goes rock climbing

e. He has free time

f. They go swimming

g. My parents do sport

h. She plays football often

Question Skills 3: Clothes/Free time/Weather

1. Translate into English

a. Quina roba portes quan fa fred?

b. Quin temps fa on vius?

c. Què fas en el teu temps lliure?

d. Fas esport?

e. Amb quina freqüència fas bàsquet?

f. Per què no t'agrada el futbol?

g. On fas escalada?

h. Quin és el teu esport preferit?

2. Complete with the missing question word:

a. _____________ vius?

b. __________ esport fas?

c. __________ esport prefereixes?

d. ____________ fas natació?

e. __________ compres les teves sabates?

f. ___________ t'agrada fer en el teu temps lliure?

g. Amb ___________ jugues a tennis?

h. Amb ________ freqüència fas equitació?

i. ________ ________ no jugues amb mi? :(

3. Split questions

Què fas	escalada?
Amb qui	portes quan fa fred?
Per	en el teu temps lliure?
On fas	roba nova?
Què	jugues a escacs?
Quin és	quan fa calor?
Tens molta	el teu esport preferit?
Quina roba portes	què no t'agrada el tennis?

4. Translate into Catalan

a. What?

b. Where?

c. How?

d. When?

e. Why?

f. How much? (m. sg)

g. How many? (f. pl)

h. From where?

i. Which?

5. Write the questions to these answers

a. Quan fa fred porto abric

b. El cap de setmana faig esport

c. Vaig al gimnàs a les cinc de la tarda

d. Tinc dos xandalls

e. Jugo a tennis amb la meva tieta

f. Faig natació a la piscina a prop de casa meva

g. Gairebé mai faig escalada

6. Translate into Catalan

a. Where do you play tennis?

b. What do you do when you have free time?

c. How many shoes do you have?

d. What is your favourite hobby?

e. Do you do sport often?

f. At what time do you do your homework?

UNIT 16
Talking about my daily routine

In this unit you will learn how to say:

- What you do every day
- At what time you do it
- Sequencing events/actions (e.g. using 'then', 'finally')

You will revisit:
- Numbers
- Free time activities
- Nationalities
- Clothes
- Hair and eyes
- Food
- Jobs

UNIT 16
Talking about my daily routine

Cap allà a les... *At around...*		**m'aixeco** *I get up*	
A... *At*		**descanso** *I rest*	
...la una *1*		**dino** *I have lunch*	
...les cinc *5*		**em rento les dents** *I brush my teeth*	
...les sis *6*			
...les set *7*		**em vesteixo** *I get dressed*	
...les vuit i cinc *8.05*	**del matí** *in the morning*		
...les vuit i deu *8.10*		**esmorzo** *I have breakfast*	**llavors** *then*
...les vuit i quart *8.15*			
...un quart de nou *8.15*	**de la tarda** *in the afternoon*	**faig els meus deures** *I do my homework*	
...les vuit i vint *8.20*			
...les vuit i vint-i-cinc *8.25*		**jugo a l'ordinador** *I play on the computer*	**després** *after*
...les vuit i mitja *8.30*	**del vespre** *in the evening*	**miro la tele** *I watch television*	
...dos quarts de nou *8.30*			**finalment** *finally*
...les vuit i trenta cinc *8.35*		**sopo** *I have dinner*	
...les nou menys vint *8.40*	**de la nit** *at night*	**surto de casa** *I leave my house*	
...les nou menys quart *8.45*			
...tres quarts de nou *8.45*		**torno a casa** *I go back home*	
...les nou menys deu *8.50*			
...lcs nou menys cinc *8.55*		**vaig a dormir** *I go to sleep*	
Al migdia *12 pm*		**vaig a l'escola en autobús** *I go to school by bus*	
A mitjanit *12 am*			

Unit 16. Talking about my daily routine: VOCAB BUILDING (Part 1)

1. Match

M'aixeco	I have lunch
Vaig a l'escola	I have dinner
Vaig a dormir	I get up
Dino	I have breakfast
Sopo	I rest
Esmorzo	I go to school
Descanso	I go back home
Torno a casa	I go to sleep

2. Translate into English

a. M'aixeco a les sis del matí

b. Vaig a dormir a les onze de la nit

c. Dino al migdia

d. Esmorzo a les sis del matí

e. Torno a casa a les tres i mitja de la tarda

f. Sopo cap allà a les vuit de la tarda

g. Miro la tele

h. Escolto música

i. Surto de casa a les sis del matí

3. Complete with the missing words

a. ___________ a l'escola — *I go to school*

b. ___________ de casa — *I leave the house*

c. ___________ a casa — *I come back home*

d. ___________ la tele — *I watch television*

e. ___________ els meus deures *I do my homework*

f. ___________ música — *I listen to music*

g. ___________ a l'ordinador — *I play on the computer*

h. ____________ al migdia — *I have lunch at noon*

4. Complete with the missing letters

a. ____escanso — *I rest*

b. ____orno a ___asa — *I go back home*

c. ____scolto música — *I listen to music*

d. ___smorzo — *I have breakfast*

e. ___opo — *I have dinner*

f. ___aig a l'escola — *I go to school*

g. M' ___ixeco — *I get up*

h. ___aig a dormir — *I go to sleep*

i. __ino — *I have lunch*

5. Faulty translation: spot and correct (in the English) the translation mistakes

a. Descanso una mica — *I shower a bit*

b. Vaig a dormir a mitjanit — *I go to sleep at noon*

c. Faig els meus deures — *I do your homework*

d. Dino — *I have lunch*

e. Vaig a l'escola — *I come back from school*

f. Torno a casa — *I leave the house*

g. Miro la tele — *I watch television*

h. Surto de casa — *I leave school*

i. Em rento les dents — *I wash my hands*

6. Translate the following times into Catalan (add *del matí / de la tarda / de la nit* where appropriate)

a. At 6.30 a.m.

b. At 7.30 a.m.

c. At 8.20 p.m.

d. At midday

e. At 9.20 a.m.

f. At 11.00 p.m.

g. At midnight

h. At 5.15 p.m.

Unit 16. Talking about my daily routine: VOCAB BUILDING (Part 2)

1. Complete the table

Vaig a dormir	
	I brush my teeth
M'aixeco	
	I go back home
A les vuit i quart	
Dino	
	I have dinner
Escolto música	
	I leave the house
Esmorzo	
Descanso	
	I do my homework
Em vesteixo	

2. Complete with the missing word

a. A les set i ___________   *At seven thirty*

b. Cap a ________ cinc   *At about 5.00*

c. A les vuit del _________   *At 8.00 a.m.*

d. Al _____________   *At noon*

e. A les ________ i quart   *At 11.15*

f. A les tres ________ vint   *At 2.40*

g. A _____________   *At midnight*

h. Cap ___ les quatre   *At about 4.00*

i. ______ a les set   *At about 7.00*

j. A las vuit menys _________   *At 7.55*

cinc	mitja	les	matí	migdia
onze	cap	menys	a	mitjanit

3. Translate into English

a. A dos quarts de nou ______ ***At 8.30*** ______

b. A les nou i quart _________________

c. A les deu menys cinc _________________

d. Al migdia _____________________________

e. A mitjanit ___________________________

f. A les onze menys cinc _________________

g. A les dotze i vint _____________________

4. Complete

a. A l____ c________ i m_________   *At 5.30*

b. A l___ v______ i q________   *At 8.15*

c. Al m_____________   *At noon*

d. A tres q________ d____ v________   *At 7.45*

e. A m_____________   *At midnight*

f. A dos q________ d____ d________   *At 11.30*

g. C____ a la u______   *At about 1.00*

5. Translate into Catalan

a. I go to school at around 8

b. I come back home at around 3

c. I have dinner at 7.30

d. I do my homework at around 5.30

e. I have breakfast at 6.45

f. I go to sleep at midnight

g. I have lunch at midday

Unit 16. Talking about my daily routine: READING (Part 1)

Em dic Hiroto. Soc japonès. La meva rutina diària és molt senzilla. Normalment m'aixeco cap a les sis. Després em dutxo i em vesteixo, i esmorzo amb el meu pare i el meu germà petit. Després em rento les dents i em pentino. Cap a les set i mitja surto de casa i vaig a l'escola. Vaig en bici. Torno a casa cap a les quatre. Després descanso una mica. Normalment miro la tele. Llavors vaig al parc amb els meus amics fins a les sis. De les sis a les set i mitja faig els meus deures. Després, a les vuit, sopo amb la meva família. No menjo gaire, només una hamburguesa. Després miro una pel·lícula a la tele, i cap a les onze vaig a dormir. **Hiroto, 10 anys. Japó**

Em dic Gregorio. Soc mexicà. La meva rutina diària és molt senzilla. Normalment m'aixeco a les sis i quart. Després em dutxo i esmorzo amb els meus dos germans. Després em rento les dents i preparo la motxilla.
Cap a les set vaig a l'escola. Vaig a l'escola a peu. Torno a casa cap a les tres i mitja. Després em relaxo una mica. Normalment miro les xarxes socials, miro una sèrie a Netflix o xerro amb els meus amics per WhatsApp. De les cinc a les sis faig els deures. Després, a les set i mitja, sopo amb la meva família. Menjo arròs o una amanida. Després miro la tele i, cap a les onze i mitja, vaig a dormir. **Gregorio, 14 anys. Mèxic**

Em dic Andreas. Soc alemany. La meva rutina diària és molt senzilla. Normalment m'aixeco aviat, cap a les cinc. Vaig a córrer i després em dutxo i em vesteixo. Després, cap a les sis i mitja, esmorzo fruita amb la meva mare i la meva germana. Després em rento les dents i preparo la meva motxilla. Cap a les set i quart surto de casa i vaig a l'escola. Torno a casa cap a les tres i mitja. Després descanso una mica. Normalment miro la tele o parlo amb els meus amics pel mòbil. De les sis a les vuit faig els meus deures. Després, a les vuit i quart, sopo amb la meva família. No menjo gaire. Després jugo a la Play fins a la mitjanit, i finalment vaig a dormir. **Andreas, 15 anys. Alemanya**

1. Answer the following questions about Hiroto

a. Where is he from?

b. At what time does he get up?

c. Who does he have breakfast with?

d. At what time does he leave the house?

e. Until what time does he stay at the park?

f. How does he go to school?

2. Find the Catalan for the following in Hiroto's text

a. At around eleven

b. With my friends

c. I go by bike

d. I go to the park

e. I shower and dress

f. I don't eat much

g. From six to seven

h. I do my homework

3. Complete the statements below about Andreas

a. He gets up at _______________________________________

b. He comes back from school at _____________________

c. For breakfast he eats _______________________________

d. He has breakfast with _______________________________

e. After getting up he _______________ and then showers

f. Usually he _______________________________ until midnight

g. After breakfast he brushes his teeth and then

____.

4. Find the Catalan for the following in Gregorio's text

a. I am Mexican

b. I shower

c. With my two brothers

d. I relax a bit

e. I eat rice or salad

f. I look at the social networks

g. I have dinner

Unit 16. Talking about my daily routine: READING (Part 2)

Em dic Yang. Tinc dotze anys. Soc xinès. La meva rutina diària és molt senzilla. Normalment m'aixeco cap a les sis i mitja. Després em dutxo i em vesteixo. Després esmorzo amb la meva mare i el meu germà, Li Wei. Després em rento les dents i preparo la motxilla. Cap a les set i mitja surto de casa i vaig a l'escola. Torno a casa cap a les quatre. Després descanso una mica. Normalment miro la tele, escolto música o llegeixo els meus còmics preferits. De les sis a les set i mitja faig els meus deures. Després, a les vuit, sopo amb la meva família. No menjo gaire. Després miro una pel·lícula a la tele, i cap a les onze vaig a dormir. **Yang. 12 anys. Xina**

Em dic Anna. Soc italiana. La meva rutina diària és molt senzilla. Normalment m'aixeco a les sis i quart. Després em rento i esmorzo amb la meva germana gran. Després em rento les dents i preparo la motxilla. Cap a les set vaig a l'escola en autobús. Torno a casa cap a les dos i mitja. Després descanso una mica. Normalment miro les xarxes socials, miro la tele o llegeixo revistes. De les cinc a les set faig els deures. A les vuit, sopo amb la meva família. Menjo fruita o una amanida. Després llegeixo una novel·la i cap allà a les onze i mitja vaig a dormir. **Anna. 14 anys. Itàlia**

Em dic Kim, soc anglesa. Tinc quinze anys. La meva rutina diària és molt senzilla. Normalment m'aixeco aviat, cap a dos quarts de sis. Faig exercici i després em rento i em vesteixo. Tot seguit, cap a les set, esmorzo amb la meva mare i la meva germanastra. Després em rento les dents i preparo la motxilla. Cap a les set i mitja surto de casa i vaig a l'escola. Torno a casa a les tres i descanso una mica. Normalment, escolto música o xerro amb els meus amics per WhatsApp. De les sis a les vuit faig els deures. Després, a un quart de nou, sopo amb la meva família i miro una pel·lícula a la tele fins a la mitjanit. Finalment, me'n vaig a dormir.
Kim. 15 anys. Anglaterra

1. Find the Catalan for the following in Yang's text

a. I am Chinese

b. My daily routine

c. I shower

d. Very simple

e. At around 7.30

f. I don't eat much

g. I watch television

h. I go to school

i. I do my homework

j. From six to seven

2. Translate these items from Kim's text

a. I am English

b. Generally

c. At around 5.30

d. With my mum and stepsister

e. I go back home

f. I have dinner with my family

g. I rest a bit

h. I brush my teeth

3. Answer the following questions on Anna's text

a. What nationality is Anna?

b. At what time does she get up?

c. What three things does she do after school?

d. How does she go to school?

e. Who does she have breakfast with?

f. At what time does she go to bed?

g. What does she eat for dinner?

h. What does she read before going to bed?

4. Find someone who

a. ...has breakfast with their older sister

b. ...doesn't watch television at night

c. ...reads magazines

d. ...gets up at 5.30am

e. ...has breakfast with their brother and mother

f. ...chats with their friends on the internet after school

g. ...does exercise in the morning

Unit 16. Talking about my daily routine: WRITING

1. Split sentences

Vaig a l'escola	casa
Torno a	deures
Faig els meus	en autobús
Miro	la tele
Jugo a l'	a mitjanit
M'aixeco a	de casa
Vaig a dormir	les sis
Surto	ordinador

2. Complete with the correct option

a. M'aixeco a _________ set del matí

b. Faig els _________ deures

c. Miro _________ tele

d. Jugo a l' _______________

e. Vaig a _____________ a mitjanit

f. Torno _________ casa

g. Surto de ___________

h. Vaig a l' _________ en autobús

a	dormir	les	escola
la	meus	casa	ordinador

3. Spot and correct the mistakes

a. Vaig a escola en bici

b. M'aixeco a la set i mitja

c. Surto de casa a vuit

d. Torno a l'casa

e. Vaig l'escola en autobús

f. Vaig a dormir cap allà onze

g. Sopo a les vuit menos quarto

h. Faig els meus deures a les cinc i media

4. Complete the words

a. qu_________ *quarter*

b. mi_________ *half*

c. a l_____ d_____ *at 10*

d. c _______ a l_______ *at around*

e. a l_______ v_________ *at 8*

f. v_________ *twenty*

g. ll___________ *then*

h. d____________ *I have lunch*

i. t_____________ *I come back*

j. j____________ *I play*

5. Guided writing: write 3 short paragraphs in the first person (I) using the details below

Person	Gets up	Showers	Goes to school	Comes back home	Watches TV	Has dinner	Goes to bed
Hans	6.30	7.00	8.05	3.30	6.00	8.10	11.10
Pierre	6.40	7.10	7.40	4.00	6.30	8.15	12.00
Mary	7.15	7.30	8.00	3.15	6.40	8.20	11.30

Revision Quickie 5: Clothes / Food / Free Time / Describing people

1. Match: clothes

Una bufanda (1)	A baseball cap
Una jaqueta	A skirt
Una gorra	A dress
Una corbata	A shirt
Una faldilla	A T-shirt
Un vestit	Jeans
Una samarreta	A jacket
Una camisa	Socks
Uns texans	Trousers
Uns mitjons	A scarf (1)
Uns pantalons	A tie

2. Write a word for each of the cues below

A fruit starting with **P**	poma
A vegetable starting with **B**	
A dairy product starting with **F**	
A meat starting with **C**	
A drink starting with **S**	
A drink made using lemons **LL**	
A sweet dessert starting with **P**	
A fruit starting with **C**	

3. Complete the translations below

a. Shoes: *sab_______________*

b. Hat: *ba_______________*

c. Hair: *ca_______________*

d. Curly: *arr_______________*

e. Blue: *bl_______________*

f. Milk: *ll_______________*

g. Water: *a_______________*

h. Drink: *be_______________*

i. Job: *tr_______________*

j. Clothes: *ro_______________*

4. Categories: clothes, colours, food, jobs

Roba	Colors	Feines	Menjar

camisa	blau	metgessa	bombera
carn	vermell	pintor	pollastre
vestit	cuiner	formatge	corbata
taronja	barret	arròs	groc

5. Match questions and answers

Quina és la teva professió preferida?	Un xandall
Quin color t'agrada més?	El de dibuix
Quin tipus de carn no t'agrada?	La d'advocat
Què portes normalment al gimnàs?	Jugar a escacs
Quin és el teu professor preferit?	El blau
Quina és la teva beguda preferida?	La de porc
Què t'agrada fer en el teu temps lliure?	El suc de fruita

6. Complete with *faig, vaig* or *jugo*

a. No ____________ esport

b. Mai ____________ a bàsquet

c. ____________ al gimnàs sovint

d. ____________ peses cada día

e. Sempre ____________ a l'ordinador

f. No ____________ a la piscina avui

7. Complete with the missing verb

a. _____________ suc de fruita.

b. M' _________________ les maduixes.

c. Després de fer els deures _______ al gimnàs o _________ a videojocs.

d. _________________ molt esport.

e. Al matí no _________________ gaire. Només dues torrades.

f. El meu pare ___________ d'enginyer. Jo no ___________ encara. _______ estudiant.

g. No m' ____________ mirar dibuixos animats. _________ mirar sèries a Netflix.

h. Al matí m' ____________ a les sis.

aixeco	jugo	encanten	treballo
faig	vaig	prefereixo	soc
treballa	bec	agrada	esmorzo

10. Complete the translation

a. El meu germà és _________________

My brother is a fireman

b. No _________________. Soc _________________

I don't work. I am a student

c. De tant en tant __________ al cine amb el meu pare
From time to time I go to the cinema with my father

d. Mai ___________ la tele *I never watch tv*

e. No _________________ als meus professors

I don't hate my teachers

f. Els meus pares són _________________

My parents are strict

g. Mai _________ a _____________
I never go jogging

8. Translate the time markers

a. Mai:

b. De tant en tant:

c. Sempre:

d. Cada dia:

e. Poques vegades:

f. Una vegada a la setmana:

g. Dues vegades al mes:

9. Split sentences: relationships

Em porto bé amb	els meus avis
No em porto	la meva mare
Els meus pares	un pesat
M'encanten	bé amb el meu pare
El meu germà és	d'art és molt bo
El meu professor	són generosos
La meva xicota és molt	perquè són estressants
Odio els exàmens	amable
No aguanto	agrada molt
El meu gos m'	a la meva germana

11. Translate into Catalan

a. I play tennis every day

b. I wear a jacket sometimes

c. I go to the gym often

d. I don't watch cartoons

e. I get up at around 6 a.m.

f. I shower twice a day

UNIT 17
Describing my house:
- indicating where it is located
- saying what I like/dislike about it

In this unit you will learn how to say in Catalan

- Where your house/apartment is located
- What your favourite room is
- What you like to do in each room
- The present indicative of key reflexive verbs in -AR

You will revisit:
- Adjectives to describe places
- Frequency markers
- Countries

Visc en una casa *I live in a … house*	**bonica** *beautiful* **gran** *big* **lletja** *ugly* **nova** *new* **petita** *small* **vella** *old*	**als afores** *on the outskirts* **al camp** *in the countryside* **al centre de la ciutat** *in the city centre*	**A casa meva hi ha quatre/cinc/sis habitacions** *in my house there are 4/5/6 rooms* **La meva habitació preferida és** *my favourite room is*	**el bany** *the bathroom* **el jardí** *the garden* **el menjador** *the dining room*
Visc en un pis *I live in a … flat*	**bonic** *beautiful* **gran** *big* **lleig** *ugly* **nou** *new* **petit** *small* **vell** *old*	**a la costa** *on the coast* **a la muntanya** *in the mountain* **a una zona residencial** *in a residential area*	**M'agrada treballar a/al** *I like to work in* **M'agrada relaxar-me a/al** *I like to relax in* **Sempre em dutxo a/al** *I always shower in*	**la cuina** *the kitchen* **la meva habitació** *my bedroom* **la sala d'estar** *the living room* **la terrassa** *the terrace*

Unit 17. Describing my house: VOCABULARY BUILDING PART 1

1. Match

visc en	a flat
una casa	new
un pis	residential
gran	area
nou	I live in
el camp	a house
zona	big
residencial	the countryside

3. Complete with the missing words

a. Visc ____ la costa

I live on the coast

b. M' ____________ la meva casa

I like my house

c. ______ en una casa vella però ______

I live in an old but pretty house

d. M'agrada ____________ a la sala d'estar

I like to relax in the living room

e. La ________ casa està als ____________

My house is on the outskirts

2. Translate into English

a. Visc en una casa petita i vella

b. Visc en un pis gran i nou

c. El meu pis està als afores

d. La meva casa està al camp

e. La meva habitació preferida és la meva

f. M'agrada la cuina

g. M'agrada treballar a la sala d'estar

h. Sempre em dutxo al bany

i. M'agrada relaxar-me al jardí

4. Complete the words

a. una c_______ *a house*
b. ll____________ *ugly*
c. n____________ *new*
d. v____________ *old*
e. g____________ *big*
f. ____________ *in*

g. la c____________ *the coast*
h. les a____________ *the outskirts*
i. el c____________ *the centre*
j. el j____________ *the garden*
k. la t____________ *the terrace*
l. l'____________ *the room*

5. Categories: sort the words into the categories

a. **sempre**	i. gran
b. relaxar–me	j. a vegades
c. mai	k. menjador
d. bonic	l. camp
e. nou	m. petit
f. muntanya	n. treballar
g. em dutxo	o. costa
h. habitació	p. visc

Time phrases	Nouns	Verbs	Adjectives
a.			

6. Translate into Catalan

a. I live in an old flat

b. I live in a new house

c. In the town centre

d. I like to relax in the living room

e. I always shower in the bathroom

f. I live in a residential area

g. My favourite room is the kitchen

Unit 17. Describing my house: VOCABULARY BUILDING PART 2

1. Match

visc en	costa
una casa	residencial
a la	un pis
un pis	bonica
al	modern
una zona	relaxar–me
sempre em	centre
m'agrada	dutxo

2. Complete with the missing word

a. No m'agrada _____________ — *I don't like to work*

b. És petit però ___________ — *It is small but pretty*

c. Està al __________ de la ciutat — *It is in the town centre*

d. Està als _____________ — *It is on the outskirts*

e. Visc en una ________ gran — *I live in a big house*

f. A una __________ residencial — *In a residential area*

g. La meva ___________ preferida és… — *My favourite room is…*

h. Em relaxo al _____________ — *I relax in the garden*

i. Estudio al meu _______________ — *I study in my bedroom*

j. __________ quatre habitacions — *There are four rooms*

zona	treballar	afores	centre	jardí
casa	dormitori	bonic	habitació	hi ha

3. Translate into English

a. Visc a una casa petita

b. Està a la costa

c. Un pis gran però lleig

d. Està a una zona residencial

e. A casa meva hi ha cinc habitacions

f. M'agrada treballar al menjador

g. M'agrada relaxar-me

h. Visc a una casa a la costa

i. Visc als afores de la ciutat

4. Broken words

a. M'agrada re_______________ — *I like to relax*

b. Visc a la m_______________ — *I live in the mountain*

c. El centre de la ci___________ — *The city centre*

d. Mai em d________________… — *I never shower…*

e. …al j______________ — *…in the garden*

f. La meva habitació p_________ — *My favourite room*

g. El meu do________________ — *My bedroom*

5. *El, La, L ',* or *Els*?

a. ______**La**______ costa

b. _____________ camp

c. _____________ menjador

d. _____________ sala d'estar

e. _____________ ciutat

f. _____________ jardí

g. _____________ bany

h. _____________ habitació

i. _____________ afores

j. _____________ zona

6. Bad translation: spot any fix the translation mistakes

a. Visc en una casa a la costa – *I live in a flat on the coast*

b. La meva habitació preferida és la cuina
   My favourite room is the dining room

c. M'agrada relaxar-me a la meva habitació
   I like to study in my bedroom

d. Visc en un pis a una zona residencial
   I live in a house in a residential area

e. M'agrada la meva casa perquè és gran i bonica
   I don't like my house because it is big and ugly

f. M'agrada treballar al menjador – *I like to work in the kitchen*

g. A casa meva hi ha quatre habitacions
   In my house there are fourteen rooms

Unit 17. Describing my house: READING

Em dic Dante. Soc d'Itàlia. Visc en una casa gran i bonica a la costa, m'agrada molt. A casa meva hi ha deu habitacions i la meva habitació preferida és la cuina. M'agrada cuinar a la cuina amb la meva mare. Sempre em desperto a les set, em dutxo al bany i després em vesteixo al meu dormitori. La meva amiga Bea viu en una casa petita a la muntanya. La Bea és molt graciosa i treballadora. No li agrada la seva casa perquè és molt petita. **Dante, 8 anys. Itàlia**

Em dic Miquel i soc de Vic, a Catalunya. La meva casa està al centre de la ciutat, però visc molt lluny de la costa. A casa parlo català i castellà.
Visc en una casa petita, nova i molt bonica. Hi ha sis habitacions i també tinc un jardí molt gran. El meu cavall viu al jardí. Es diu Dani (el cavall, no el jardí). La meva habitació preferida a casa és el menjador perquè m'agrada molt menjar!
M'agrada relaxar-me a la meva habitació. Sempre miro dibuixos animats i sèries a Netflix. També m'agrada llegir i treballar aquí, quan tinc deures de l'escola, per exemple. **Miquel, 17 anys. Vic**

Em dic Gonzalo. Soc espanyol i visc en una casa molt vella però molt bonica al camp, a Andalusia. M'encanta la meva casa! A casa meva hi ha cinc habitacions, i la meva habitació preferida és la sala d'estar. Cada dia, després de l'escola, m'agrada relaxar-me a la sala d'estar i mirar la tele amb la meva germana. **Gonzalo, 9 anys. Espanya**

1. Answer the following questions about Dante

a. Where is he from?

b. What is his house like?

c. How many rooms are there in his house?

d. Which is his favourite room?

e. Where does he get dressed?

f. Where does Bea live?

g. Does she like her house? Why?

2. Find the Catalan for the following in Miquel's text

a. my house is in the centre

b. I live very far…

c. I speak Catalan and Spanish

d. I also have a garden

e. I really like to eat

f. he lives in the garden

g. I like to relax

h. I like to read and work

Em dic Lola, soc de França. Sempre em desperto a les cinc del matí perquè visc lluny de l'escola, als afores de la ciutat. Visc en un pis en un edifici molt vell. El pis és molt vell i una mica lleig, però m'agrada. M'agrada relaxar-me a la meva habitació. A vegades llegeixo llibres i escolto música a Spotify. El meu dormitori és la meva habitació preferida. **Lola, 13 anys. França**

4. Find the Catalan for the following in Lola's text

a. I am from France

b. I always wake up at 5

c. I live far from school

d. The flat is very old

e. …and a bit ugly

f. But I like it

g. Sometimes I read books

3. Find someone who

a. …lives far from school

b. …speaks two languages

c. …has a really really big house

d. …watches TV with his sister

e. …has a big pet that lives outside the house

f. …listens to music on a streaming platform

g. …is a foodie (loves food)

h. …has a friend that doesn't like their own house

Unit 17. Describing my house: TRANSLATION

1. Gapped translation

a. Visc als afores – *I live on the* ______________

b. La meva casa és molt gran però una mica lletja

   My house is ________ *big but* ___ ______ *ugly*

c. Està a la muntanya – *It is in the* ______________

d. Visc al centre ______ ______ ____________

   I live in the city centre

e. A casa meva ______ ______ cinc habitacions

   In my house there are five rooms

f. No m'agrada gens la ____________ perquè és ________

   I don't like at all the kitchen because it's ugly

2. Translate to English

a. la costa

b. un pis

c. visc a

d. el centre

e. de la ciutat

f. la meva habitació preferida

g. m'agrada relaxar-me

h. el meu dormitori

i. la sala d'estar

3. Translate into English

a. Visc en un pis petit i lleig

b. La meva casa és moderna però bastant bonica

c. El meu pis és vell però m'agrada molt

d. Visc en una casa a la costa

e. A casa meva hi ha cinc habitacions

f. La meva habitació preferida és el meu dormitori

4. Translate into Catalan

a. Big: G____________________

b. Small: P____________________

c. Outskirts: A____________________

d. Coast: C____________________

e. Area: Z____________________

f. Residential: R____________________

g. Ugly: LL____________________

h. Room: H____________________

i. There are: H____________________

j. Old: V____________________

5. Translate into Catalan

a. I live in a small house

b. In the city centre

c. In my house there are...

d. Seven rooms

e. My favourite room is...

f. The living room

g. I like to relax in my bedroom

h. And I like to work in the living room

i. I live in a small and old flat

j. In a residential area

Grammar Time 14: VIURE – to live

(Jo) Visc *I live* **(Tu) Vius** *you* **(Ell) Viu** *he* **(Ella) Viu** *she*	**en una casa**	**acollidora** *cosy* **bonica** *beautiful* **lletja** *ugly* **gran** *big* **nova** *new* **petita** *small* **vella** *old*	**als afores** *on the outskirts* **al camp** *in the countryside* **al centre de la ciutat** *in the city centre*
(Nosaltres) Vivim *we* **(Vosaltres) Viviu** *you (plural)* **(Ells) Viuen** *they -masculine/mixed-* **(Elles) Viuen** *they -female-*	**en un pis**	**acollidor** *cosy* **bonic** *beautiful* **lleig** *ugly* **gran** *big* **nou** *new* **petit** *small* **vell** *old*	**a la costa** *on the coast* **a la muntanya** *in the mountain* **a una zona residencial** *in a residential area*

1. Match

viuen	I live
vivim	you live
viu	he/she lives
visc	we live
viviu	you guys live
vius	they live

3. Complete with the correct form of *viure*

a. La meva mare i jo _______________ a

Barcelona. El meu pare ___________ a

Sabadell.

b. (vosaltres) On ______________?

c. Jo _________ a Londres. El meu germà

____________ a París.

d. Els meus tiets ____________ als Estats Units.

e. La meva xicota no ___________ aquí.

f. (jo) ____________ en una casa molt gran

g. (tu) ____________ en una casa enorme!

5. Complete the translation

a. My siblings live in the countryside

Els meus ____________ _________ *al* ___________

b. I live in a flat. _________ *en un* _________

c. My mother doesn't live with my father

La meva mare no ________ ______ *el meu pare*

d. We live on the outskirts

____________ *a les* ____________

e. Where do you live? *On* __________?

f. They live in a small house

(Ells) ________ *en una* ______ __________

2. Complete with the correct form of *viure*

a. __________ en una casa bonica

   I live in a beautiful house

b. On __________ – *Where do you (singular) live?*

c. ______________ a Londres des de fa tres anys

   I have lived in London for three years

d. ____________ en una casa a la costa

   He/she lives in a house on the coast

e. __________ en una casa o a un pis?

   Do you live in a house or in a flat?

f. ____________ en un pis antic

   They live in an old flat

g. ____________ als afores

   We live on the outskirts

h. El meu pare ___________ en una granja

   My father lives on a farm

4. Spot and correct the mistakes

a. (jo) No vius al centre de la ciutat

b. Els meus pares vivim aquí

c. La meva xicota viuen en un pis a la costa

d. La meva mare i jo viviu als afores

e. Els meus germans no viu amb nosaltres

f. El meu avi matern visc amb nosaltres

6. Translate into Catalan

a. My parents and I live in a cosy house

b. My mother lives in a small house on the coast

c. My cousins live in a beautiful house in the countryside

d. My girlfriend lives in a modern flat in the centre

e. My sisters live in an old flat on the ouskirts

f. My best friend Pep lives in a spacious flat near the town centre

Grammar Time 15: Reflexives (Part 1)

<table>
<tr><td colspan="2" align="center">USEFUL VOCABULARY</td></tr>
<tr><td>Afaitar–se</td><td>To shave</td></tr>
<tr><td>Banyar–se</td><td>To bathe</td></tr>
<tr><td>Queixar-se</td><td>To complain</td></tr>
<tr><td>Dutxar-se</td><td>To shower</td></tr>
<tr><td>Dir-se</td><td>To be called</td></tr>
<tr><td>Rentar-se</td><td>To wash</td></tr>
<tr><td>Aixecar-se</td><td>To get up</td></tr>
<tr><td>Relaxar–se</td><td>To rest</td></tr>
<tr><td>Pentinar-se</td><td>To comb one's hair</td></tr>
<tr><td>Preparar–se</td><td>To get ready</td></tr>
</table>

Present Indicative of AR verbs ending in SE

	Rentar-se	Afaitar-se
jo	em rento	m'afaito
tu	et rentes	t'afaites
ell / **ella**	es renta	s'afaita
nosaltres	ens rentem	ens afaitem
vosaltres	us renteu	us afaiteu
ells / **elles**	es renten	s'afaiten

1. Complete with the pronoun

a. (ells) _____ aixequen

b. (jo) _____ dutxo

c. (ella) _____ queixa

d. (nosaltres) _____ rentem

e. (ell) _____ renta les dents

f. (nosaltres) _____ pentinem

g. (elles) _____ relaxen

h. (elles) _____ arreglen

2. Complete with the correct form of the verb

a. (ella – rentar-se) _____ _____________ les dents

b. (nosaltres – dutxar-se) _______ _______________ ràpid

c. (ell – cansar–se) _____ ___________ molt a les classes
   d'educació física

d. (ell – afaitar-se) mai _______ _________________

e. (ella – relaxar–se) mai _______ _________________

f. (ells – aixecar-se) ______ __________________ aviat

g. (ell – queixar–se) sempre _____ ______________

3. Translate into English

a. M'aixeco cap a les sis, però la meva germana s'aixeca cap a les set. Jo em dutxo de seguida, però la meva germana mai es dutxa al matí.

b. El meu germà es relaxa abans d'anar a l'escola. Ell sempre es mira al mirall.

c. M'afaito gairebé cada dia. El meu pare s'afaita cada dia.

d. Els meus pares s'aixequen més aviat que jo. Després es renten i esmorzen abans que nosaltres.

e. El meu pare és calb, per tant mai es pentina.

f. La meva mare té molts cabells. Ella es pentina durant mitja hora abans de sortir de casa.

g. No tenim cap banyera a casa meva, per tant ens dutxem, però no ens banyem.

h. Jo em rento les dents cinc vegades al dia. En canvi, el meu germà es renta les dents només una vegada al dia.

Jo m'aixeco després del meu pare, mitja hora més tard, cap a les sis i mitja. Em rento, em dutxo, m'afaito, em pentino i finalment em vesteixo i vaig a la cuina. Esmorzo sol. Menjo cereals amb llet, torrades amb melmelada i prenc un cafè amb llet. Després em rento les dents, m'arreglo per anar a l'escola, i cap a les set surto de casa.
Marc, 14 anys. Reus

5. Find the Catalan for the following in Marc's text

a. I get up

b. I wash

c. I comb my hair

d. I brush my teeth

e. I get ready

f. I shave

g. I shower

h. I drink

i. I leave the house

6. Complete

a. Em dutx__   *I shower*

b. S'afait__   *He shaves*

c. Ens dut_ _ _   *We shower*

d. Us ren_ _ _   *You guys wash*

e. Em prepar__   *I prepare myself*

f. Es pent_ _ _ _   *They comb their hair*

g. Em rent_ les dents *I brush my teeth*

h. Es ban_ _ _   *They bathe*

8. Translate into Catalan

a. Normally, I shower at seven o'clock

b. He never brushes his teeth

c. We shave three times a week

d. They get up early

e. He never combs his hair

f. I don't bathe

g. We prepare ourselves for school

h. They never relax

4. Find the Catalan for the following in Arnau's text

a. They get up

b. My father gets up

c. He showers

d. He gets ready

e. My mother gets up

f. She goes to work

g. He shaves

h. She combs her hair

Els meus pares s'aixequen molt aviat. El meu pare s'aixeca cap allà a les cinc i mitja per preparar l'esmorzar per a la meva mare i per a mi. Abans de preparar l'esmorzar, es dutxa, es vesteix, s'afaita, s'arregla i pren un cafè mirant la tele. La meva mare s'aixeca mitja hora més tard. Es dutxa, es pentina i es vesteix, i després esmorza amb el meu pare a la cuina. La meva mare va a treballar mitja hora més tard, cap allà a les sis i mitja.
Arnau, 12 anys. Sant Cugat

7. Complete

a. _____ _____________ a les sis

   They get up at six

b. _____ _____________ a les set

   They shave at seven

c. _____ _____________ aviat

   I get up early

d. Mai ____ _____________

   He never shaves

e. _____ _____________ les dents

   després de menjar

   We brush our teeth after eating

f. Sempre ____ _______ al mirall

   He always looks at himself in the mirror

UNIT 18
Saying what I do at home,
how often, when and where

In this unit you will learn how to provide a more detailed account of your daily activities building on the vocabulary learnt in the previous unit.

You will revisit:
- Time markers
- Reflexive verbs
- Parts of the house
- Description of people and places
- Telling the time
- Nationalities
- The verbs *fer*, *jugar* and *anar*

Unit 18
Saying what I do at home, how often, when and where

Cap a les sis del matí *At around 6 a.m.*	**em rento les dents** *I brush my teeth*	
	em vesteixo *I get dressed*	**al bany** *in the bathroom*
Sovint *Often*	**descanso** *I rest*	**a la cuina** *in the kitchen*
	escolto música *I listen to music*	
A vegades *Sometimes*	**esmorzo** *I have breakfast*	**al garatge** *in the garage*
	faig els meus deures *I do my homework*	**a l'habitació del meu germà** *in my brother's bedroom*
Quan tinc temps *When I have time*	**jugo a la Play** *I play Playstation*	
	llegeixo còmics *I read comics*	**a l'habitació dels meus pares** *in my parents' bedroom*
Dues vegades a la setmana *Twice a week*	**llegeixo revistes** *I read magazines*	**al jardí** *in the garden*
	miro la tele *I watch television*	
	miro pel·lícules *I watch films*	**al menjador** *in the dining room*
Mai *Never*	**miro sèries a Netflix** *I watch series on Netflix*	**a la meva habitació** *in my bedroom*
Normalment *Usually*	**parlo amb la meva mare** *I chat with my...*	
	preparo el menjar *I prepare food*	**a la sala d'estar** *in the living room*
Sempre *Always*	**pujo fotos a Instagram** *I upload pics to Instagram*	**a la terrassa** *in the terrace*
Cada dia *Every day*	**surto de casa** *I leave the house*	
	vaig en bici *I ride my bike*	

Unit 18. Saying what I do at home: VOCABULARY BUILDING PART 1

1. Match

Llegeixo còmics	I chat with
Miro pel·lícules	I wash
Preparo el menjar	I watch movies
Llegeixo revistes	I prepare food
Em vesteixo	I read magazines
Xerro amb	I shower
Em rento	I get dressed
Em dutxo	I read comics

2. Complete with the missing words

a. Em ___________ *I get dressed*

b. Llegeixo ___________ *I read comics*

c. Llegeixo ___________ *I read magazines*

d. Em rento les ________ *I wash my teeth*

e. Em ___________ *I shower*

f. ___________ el menjar *I prepare food*

g. _______ sèries *I watch series*

h. ___________ música *I listen to music*

i. ________ fotos a Instagram
   I upload photos to Instagram

3. Translate into English

a. Normalment em dutxo cap a les set del matí

b. Mai preparo el menjar

c. Normalment llegeixo revistes a la sala d'estar

d. Cap a les set del matí esmorzo al menjador

e. De tant en tant xerro amb la meva mare a la cuina

f. A vegades esmorzo a la cuina

g. A vegades jugo a la Play amb el meu germà

h. Sempre surto de casa a les vuit del matí

4. Complete the words

a. Em d________ *I shower*   g. Em v________ *I get dressed*

b. L________ *I read*   h. J________ *I play*

c. X________ *I chat*   i. S________ *I leave*

d. P________ *I prepare*   j. F________ *I do*

e. P________ *I upload*   k. E________ *I listen*

f. Em r________ *I wash*   l. M________ *I watch*

5. Categories: sort the items below in the categories

a. **cap a les sis**	i. em rento les dents
b. sempre	j. de tant en tant
c. mai	k. cada dia
d. la meva habitació	l. escolto música
e. miro la tele	m. llegeixo còmics
f. jugo a la Play	n. vaig en bici
g. em dutxo	o. dues vegades a la setmana
h. pujo fotos a Instagram	p. xerro per Zoom

Time phrases	Rooms in the house	Things you do in the bathroom	Free-time activities
a.			

6. Fill in the table with what activities you do in which room

Jugo a la Play	a la meva habitació
Miro la tele	
Em dutxo	
Faig els deures	
Em rento les dents	
Descanso	
Preparo el menjar	

Unit 18. Saying what I do at home: VOCABULARY BUILDING PART 2

7. Complete the table

English	Català
I get dressed	
I shower	
	Faig els deures
I upload photos	
	Surto de casa
	Xerro amb el meu germà
I rest	

8. Multiple choice quiz

	A	B	C
Mai	always	never	sometimes
A vegades	sometimes	always	never
Habitació	room	lounge	garden
Em rento	I shave	I wash	I go out
Em dutxo	I shower	I go out	I rest
Descanso	I go out	I watch	I rest
Jardí	garden	garage	kitchen
Cuina	bedroom	lounge	kitchen
Jugo	I rest	I play	I prepare
Llegeixo	I watch	I read	I play
Surto	I go out	I rest	I read
Sempre	always	never	every day

9. Anagrams: unscramble & translate

Example iMa - Mai - never

a. inaCu

b. toSur

c. xogeiLle

d. emSpre

e. ujoP tofos

f. otner mE

10. Broken words

a. La cu_____________ *Kitchen*

b. M________________ *Never*

c. A veg_____________ *Sometimes*

d. Se_______________ *Always*

e. So_______________ *Often*

f. Els c_____________ *Comics*

g. La meva h_________ *My bedroom*

h. Su_______________ *I go out*

i. X________________ *I chat*

11. Complete

a. Cap ___ l___ s_____ i mitja, e__ r______ l___
    d________ *At around seven thirty, I brush my teeth*

b. Cap a l_____ v______ i quart, e_____________
    At around a quarter past eight I have breakfast

c. A v___________ p_________ e__ m_________
    Sometimes I prepare the food

d. S_______ m______ l___ t________ mentre
    e__________
    I always watch TV when I have breakfast

e. N__________, s_______ d___ c_____ a l____ v_____
    i mitja *Generally, I leave the house at eight thirty*

f. Poques v________ ll_________ c_________
    I read comics rarely

g. Cap a l_____ c_________ f_______ e____ m______
    d___________ *At around five I do my homework*

12. Fill in the gaps from memory

a. A vegades ________ còmics

b. Sempre em _________ les dents
   després de menjar

c. _______ sèries a Netflix cada dia

d. Mai __________ revistes de moda

e. Mai ________ els meus deures

f. ________ fotos a Instagram sovint

g. El cap de setmana ________ en bici

h. _________ de casa cap a les vuit

i. ___________ música sovint

Unit 18. Saying what I do at home: READING

Em dic Fabián. Soc de Gibraltar. Tinc un gos a casa. Sempre m'aixeco aviat, cap a les cinc i quart. Després vaig al gimnàs i faig esport. Em dutxo quan torno a casa. El meu germà Xavier és molt mandrós i inactiu. S'aixeca a les set. Ell mai juga a futbol i mai fa esport, només juga a videojocs. A la tarda llegeixo còmics a la meva habitació o escolto música. Entre setmana, quan torno a casa faig els meus deures al menjador amb la meva mare. M'agrada perquè ella és molt intel·ligent i sempre m'ajuda. Finalment, vaig a dormir les nou, a la meva habitació, és clar.
Fabián. 18 anys. Gibraltar

Em dic Valentín. Soc romanès. Sempre em desperto aviat, cap a les sis i mitja. Després em dutxo i em rento les dents al bany. No esmorzo res al matí però la meva germana Valeria esmorza cereals al menjador amb el meu pare. Vaig a l'escola a peu. Torno a casa cap allà a les tres i mitja, i després em relaxo una mica. Normalment miro la tele a la sala d'estar. Després vaig a Internet, miro una sèrie a Netflix o miro vídeos de TikTok a la meva habitació. Després, a les vuit, preparo el menjar amb la meva mare a la cuina. M'encanta preparar amanides perquè són delicioses. Vaig a dormir tard, a les deu.
Valentín. 15 anys. Romania

Em dic Anna i visc als Països Baixos. Cada dia m'aixeco a les cinc del matí. Després em dutxo, i esmorzo al jardí. Surto de casa a les set i vaig a l'escola a peu. Quan torno a casa xerro per Zoom amb la meva família a Catalunya, a la meva habitació. Després vaig en bici amb els meus dos gossos.
A vegades miro dibuixos animats i pujo fotos a Instagram. El meu germà Jordi puja vídeos a TikTok dels seus balls nous. El meu germà m'agrada molt perquè és molt divertit i actiu. Balla molt bé! Sempre xerro i jugo a cartes amb ell. El Jordi és el meu millor amic al món.
Anna. 17anys. Països Baixos

1. Answer the following questions about Fabián

a. Where is he from?

b. What animal does he have?

c. What does he do after he wakes up?

d. Is Xavier sporty?

e. Where does he do his homework on weekdays?

f. Who helps him with his homework?

g. Where does he go to bed?

2. Find the Catalan for the following in Anna's text

a. I get up

b. then I shower

c. I go to school

d. by walk

e. with my family

f. uploads videos to TikTok

g. new dances

h. I always chat

3. Find someone who

a. ...wakes up earliest

b. ...gets helps with their homework from a family member

c. ...likes to watch videos of people dancing

d. ...has nothing for breakfast

e. ...has a really lazy brother

f. ...likes to prepare healthy food

g. ...has a family member that is their best friend

h. ...has a dog

4. Find the Catalan for the following in Valentín's text

a. I am Romanian

b. I wake up early

c. I have nothing for breakfast

d. My sister Valeria eats cereals

e. In the dining room

f. In the living room

g. I watch TikTok videos

Unit 18. Saying what I do at home: WRITING

1. Split sentences

Xerro	menjar
Descanso a	aviat
Preparo el	amb la meva mare
Pujo fotos	la meva habitació
Faig els meus	les dents
Em desperto molt	a Instagram
Jugo amb el meu	ordinador
Em rento	deures

2. Complete with the correct option

a. Em desperto a les sis del ___________

b. Jugo a futbol al ___________

c. Miro la tele al ___________

d. Escolto música a la meva ___________

e. Preparo el ___________ amb el meu pare

f. Em ___________ les dents

g. ___________ dibuixos animats

h. ___________ a l'escola a cavall

menjador	matí	rento	habitació
vaig	menjar	miro	jardí

3. Spot and correct the grammar and spelling mistakes

a. em dutxa al baño

b. esmorzo al cuina

c. al meu habitació

d. jugo con la ordinador

e. surto casa a vuit

f. faig meus deures

g. miro sèrias a Netflix

h. vaig al escola a peu

i. l'habitació meu germà

4. Complete the words

a. es___________ *I have breakfast*

b. la c___________ *the kitchen*

c. la meva h___________ *my bedroom*

d. el g___________ *the garage*

e. s___________ de c___________ *I leave the house*

f. a la s___________ *in the living room*

g. al m___________ *in the dining room*

h. al b___________ *in the bathroom*

i. m___________ p___________ a___

l'___________ d_____ m_____

g___________

I watch films in my brother's bedroom

5. Guided writing: write 3 short paragraphs in the first person (I) using the details below

Person	Gets up	Showers	Has breakfast	Goes to school	Afternoon activity 1	Afternoon activity 2
Gonzalo	6.15	In bathroom	Kitchen	With brother	Watch tv in living room	Prepare food in the kitchen
Albert	7.30	In shower	Dining room	With mother	Read book in bedroom	Talk to family on Zoom
Marta	6.45	In bathroom	Living room	With Uncle	Listen to music in garden	Upload photos to instagram

Grammar Time 16: JUGAR, (Part 3) FER (Part 3) ANAR (Part 2)

1. Complete with *faig, jugo* or *vaig*

a. _____________els meus deures

b. _____________a escacs

c. _____________a França

d. _____________a la piscina

e. _____________a l'ordinador

f. _____________natació

g. _____________a futbol

h. No _________res

2. Complete with the missing forms of the present indicative of the verbs below

	Fer	Anar	Jugar
jo *I*		vaig	jugo
tu *you*	fas		
ell, ella *he/she*			
nosaltres *we*			
vosaltres *you guys/ladies*	feu		jugueu
ells, elles *they*		van	

3. Complete with the appropriate verb

a. La meva mare ______ a la universitat cada dia

b. La meva germana mai _______ els seus deures

c. (nosaltres) __________ a bàsquet cada dia

d. Els meus pares no __________ gaire esport

e. Els meus germans _________ sovint a escacs

f. La meva xicota i jo __________ a l'institut a peu

g. (tu) Què _________?

h. (vosaltres) On ____________?

i. (vosaltres) Què __________?

j. El meu cosí ___________ a futbol amb nosaltres

k. Els meus tiets ________ sovint a l'estadi

l. El meu pare ____________ a tennis

m. A l'estiu, els meus pares i jo ___________ ciclisme

n. El cap de setmana els meus pares no _________ res

4. Complete with the *nosaltres* form of *jugar, fer, anar*

a. _____________a futbol

b. ___________ al cine

c. ___________ a bàsquet

d. ___________ a l'escola

e. ___________ a tennis

f. ___________ al parc

g. ___________ a cartes

h. ___________ a la piscina

i. ___________ esport

j. ___________ patinatge

k. ___________ a córrer

l. ___________ a escacs

5. Complete with the *ells/elles* form of the verbs

a. ___________ a dames

b. ___________ a l'estadi

c. ___________ escalada

d. ___________ els deures

e. ___________ surf

f. ___________ a la platja

g. ___________ a casa

h. ___________ a videojocs

i. ___________ a dormir

j. ___________ esport

k. ___________ al parc

l. ___________ a Portugal

Present Indicative of -AR reflexive verbs		
	Rentar–se	**Dutxar–se**
jo	em rento	em dutxo
tu	et rentes	et dutxes
ell **ella**	es renta	es dutxa
nosaltres	ens rentem	ens dutxem
vosaltres	us renteu	us dutxeu
ells **elles**	es renten	es dutxen

USEFUL VOCABULARY	
Afaitar–se	To shave
Banyar–se	To bathe
Rentar-se les dents	To brush the teeth
Dutxar–se	To shower
Dir-se	To be called
Rentar-se	To wash
Aixecar-se	To get up
Relaxar-se	To relax
Pentinar-se	To comb one's hair
Preparar-se	To get ready

6. Translate into Catalan

a. We play on the computer often

b. My brother never does weight lifting

c. My sister plays netball every day

d. My father never does sport

e. What job do you guys do?

f. Where do you go after school?

g. My brother and I often play chess

h. My parents and I go swimming once a week

i. My brother never goes to the market

j. My best friend goes to the stadium every Saturday

7. Complete with the correct ending

a. La meva mare es d________ Marina

b. El meu germà no es r__________

c. Em dut_______ sovint

d. El meu pare s'af_________ cada dia

e. Em dutxo i em pe____________

f. Ens aixequ_________ cap a les set

g. Quan et dut_______?

h. El meu germà mai es relax___

i. Com us di______?

8. Translate into Catalan

a. We get up at six

b. He showers, then shaves

c. I shower at around seven

d. My father never shaves

e. My brothers never wash

f. He is called Miquel

g. They have a bath

h. She gets up late

i. He doesn't brush his teeth

j. When do you rest?

THE LANGUAGE GYM

UNIT 19
My holiday plans
Talking about future plans for holidays

In this unit you will learn how to talk about:

- What you intend to do in future holidays
- Where you are going to go
- Where you are going to stay
- Who you are going to travel with
- How it will be
- Means of transport

You will revisit:

- The verb 'anar'
- Free-time activities
- Previously seen adjectives

UNIT 19
My holiday plans

Aquest estiu *This summer* **aniré de vacances a** *I will go on holiday to* **anirem de vacances a** *We will go on holiday to*	Alemanya Anglaterra Espanya França Itàlia	**en autobús** *by coach* **en avió** *by plane* **en cotxe** *by car* **en** **vaixell** *by boat*	
Passaré *I will spend* **Passarem** *We will spend*	**una setmana** *1 week* **dues setmanes** *2 weeks*	**allà** *there* **amb la meva família** *with my family*	**Serà avorrit** *it will be boring*
Em quedaré en *I will stay in* **Ens quedarem en** *We will stay in*	**un càmping** *a camping* **una casa rural** *a country house* **un hotel barat** *a cheap hotel* **un hotel de luxe** *a luxury hotel*		**Serà divertit** *it will be fun*
Aquest estiu *This summer* **Aquest cap de setmana** *This weekend*	**ballaré** *I will dance* **bussejaré** *I will go diving* **compraré records** *I will buy souvenirs* **descansaré** *I will rest* **menjaré i dormiré** *I will eat and sleep* **aniré a la platja** *I will go to the beach* **faré esport** *I will do sport* **faré turisme** *I will go sightseeing*		**Serà guai** *it will be cool*
M'agradaria *I would like to…* **Ens agradaria** *We would like to…*	**anar a comprar** *go shopping* **llogar una bici** *rent a bike* **prendre el sol** *sunbathe* **sortir de marxa** *go clubbing* **tocar l'ukelele** *play the ukulele* **visitar el centre** *visit the center*		

Unit 19. My holiday plans: VOCABULARY BUILDING

1. Match

aniré	I will spend
passaré	a camping
em quedaré	I will go
un hotel barat	it will be cool
un càmping	I'm going to stay
m'agradaria	to buy
comprar	a cheap hotel
serà guai	I would like to

2. Complete with the missing word

a. Menjar i _____________   *To eat and sleep*

b. Aniré a _____________   *I will rest*

c. M' _____________ anar a…   *I would like to go to…*

d. ______ amb els meus amics   *To play with my friends*

e. ______ quedaré a/en…   *I will stay in…*

f. __________ avorrit   *It will be boring*

g. _________________   *We will spend…*

h. Viatjaré en _________   *I will travel by plane*

i. Passaré dues setmanes ______ amb __ _______ família.
I will spend two weeks there with my family

3. Translate into English

a. Aquest estiu aniré a Grècia

b. Passaré tres setmanes allà

c. Aniré a Cuba en avió

d. Anirem de compres

e. M'agradaria sortir al centre

f. Aniré a jugar amb els meus amics

g. Ens agradaria menjar i dormir

h. Descansaré cada dia

i. Aniré a fer esport amb el meu germà

4. Broken words

a. Men___ i dorm____   *To eat and sleep*

b. Ens qu____________   *We will stay*

c. P_____________   *I spend*

d. M'__________ anar a…   *I would like to go to…*

e. Anar a la p_________   *To go to the beach*

f. A________ en bici   *To go biking*

g. P________ el sol   *To sunbathe*

h. S_______ relaxant   *It will be relaxing*

5. *Anar, jugar* or *fer*?

a. _____________ a comprar

b. _____________ al centre

c. _____________ turisme

d. _____________ a futbol

e. _____________ a cartes

f. _____________ dc vacances

g. _____________ en bici

h. _____________ esport

i. _____________ a escacs

j. _____________ a la platja

6. Bad translation: spot and fix the translation mistakes

a. Aquest estiu anirem a…   *Last summer I am go to…*

b. Aniré a Andorra amb el meu pare   *I will go to Andorra with my mother*

c. Menjaré i dormiré   *I am going to drink and sleep*

d. M'agradaria descansar molt   *I would like to rest a bit*

e. Ens quedarem en un hotel   *I am will stay in a hotel*

f. Passaré una setmana allà   *I am going to spend one week here*

g. Viatjarem en cotxe i vaixell   *I will travel by coach and barge*

h. Em quedaré a casa de la meva família   *We are stay in my family's house*

Unit 19. My holiday plans: READING (Part 1)

Em dic Oriol. Soc de Tarragona però visc a Madrid. Aquest estiu aniré de vacances al sud d'Espanya, a Cadis. Viatjaré en cotxe amb la meva parella, l'Àlex. Passarem quatre setmanes allà i anirem tots els dies a la platja. També menjarem menjar deliciós. No faré turisme perquè és molt avorrit. Prefereixo prendre el sol a la platja.
Oriol, 26 anys. Tarragona

Em dic Steven i soc de Califòrnia. La meva persona preferida és la meva dona, l'Anna. Aquest estiu viatjarem a Anglaterra i després al Quebec. A Anglaterra descansaré i llegiré llibres, i al Canadà esquiaré i sortiré amb els meus amics. L'Anna muntarà en bici i menjarà menjar deliciós, com *poutine* (semblant a les patates fregides i amb formatge). Serà fantàstic!
Steven, 34 anys. California

Em dic Marco. Soc italià, de Venècia. Aquest estiu aniré de vacances a Mèxic, en avió. Passaré dues setmanes allà, sol, i em quedaré en una caravana a la platja. Visitaré monuments, museus i galeries d'art. No m'agrada gaire l'esport, però m'encanta la cultura. Serà interessant.
Marco, 19 anys. Venècia

Em dic Magda. Soc de Polònia però visc a la Xina. Aquest estiu viatjaré a Xile amb la meva amiga Olivia. Viatjaré en vaixell perquè tinc molt temps. Passaré cinc setmanes allà i em quedaré en un hotel de luxe. M'encanta ballar, així que ballaré cada dia. També menjaré i dormiré molt. No aniré a museus perquè és molt avorrit.
Magda, 23 anys. Polònia

1. Find the Catalan for the following in Oriol's text

a. I am from…

b. But I live in…

c. I am going to travel by…

d. With my boyfriend…

e. We are going to spend…

f. Every day…

g. I am not going to…

h. I prefer to sunbathe…

2. Find the Catalan for the following in Magda's text

a. by boat…

b. I have a lot of time…

c. I am going to spend…

d. I love to dance…

e. so/therefore…

f. also…

g. it is very boring

3. Complete the following statements about Steven

a. He is from ________________

b. His favourite person is ____________

c. They will travel to ____________ and ____________

d. Steven will ____________ and ____________

e. Anna will ____________ and ____________

f. "Poutine" is made up of ____________ and ____________

4. List 8 details about Marco, in third person (he) and in English

1.

2.

3.

4.

5.

6.

7.

8.

5. Find someone who

a. …likes being out at sea for long periods

b. …loves learning about culture

c. …prefers the beach to going sightseeing

d. …has opposite interests to Marco

e. …is going to travel by car

THE LANGUAGE GYM

Unit 19. My holiday plans: READING (Part 2)

Em dic Montserrat. Soc de Barcelona. Tinc una tortuga a casa, és molt lenta i molt grassa, però m'encanta. És la meva millor amiga. Aquest estiu aniré de vacances a Màlaga, al sud d'Espanya, amb la meva família. Viatjaré en avió i després en cotxe. Passarem tres setmanes a Torremolinos i ens quedarem en un hotel de luxe. Serà molt divertit! Després anirem en cotxe a Granada i anirem a veure monuments famosos, com l'Alhambra, un palau àrab molt antic. Menjaré menjar deliciós, m'encanten les tapes. També aniré de compres cada dia i compraré roba guai.
Montserrat, 9 anys. Barcelona

Em dic Freddie. Soc de Buenos Aires, a l'Argentina. Aquest estiu aniré de vacances a la ciutat de Cuzco, al sud del Perú, amb el meu germà Brian. Viatjarem en avió i passarem dues setmanes allà. A Perú visitarem un lloc molt especial: les ruïnes inques del Machu Pichu. Serà molt impressionant i divertit. A Cuzco també farem senderisme a la muntanya. Serà dur però molt guai. Un dia m'agradaria descansar i tocar música. M'encanta cantar i al meu germà Brian li agrada molt tocar la guitarra. El nostre grup preferit es diu Queen. La meva música preferida és la música rock.
Freddie, 16 anys. Buenos Aires

Em dic Ana i visc a Granada, al sud d'Espanya. Aquest estiu viatjaré a Barcelona, a Catalunya. Viatjaré en cotxe i després en tren. Passaré dues setmanes allí i em quedaré a un hotel barat. A Barcelona m'agradaria visitar un monument molt famós que es diu la Sagrada Família. És una basílica molt gran i bonica, dissenyada per l'Antoni Gaudí. També aniré a la platja. La platja de Barcelona és una mica lletja, així que aniré en tren a un poble que es diu Sitges. La platja allà és espectacular! Tinc una amiga a Sitges que es diu Alicia. Xerrarem a la platja i prendrem el sol juntes. Serà divertit i relaxant.
Ana, 13 anys. Granada

1. Answer the following questions about Montserrat

a. Where is she from?

b. What animal does she have?

c. Who will she go on holiday with?

d. Where will they stay?

e. How will they get to Granada?

f. What is the Alhambra?

g. What will she do every day?

2. Find the Catalan in Ana's text

a. This summer

b. And then

c. Which is called

d. A basilica

e. Designed by

f. A bit ugly

g. The beach there

h. Sunbathe together

3. Find someone who

a. ...will travel south

b. ...has a brother who is a musician

c. ...has a slow moving pet

d. ...will be walking in the mountains

e. ...will visit a famous religious monument

f. ...will visit a famous palace

g. ...will visit the oldest historical site

h. ...will plan to relax on the beach

4. Find the Catalan for the following in Freddie's text

a. My brother Brian

b. The Incan ruins

c. It will be very impressive

d. It will be tough

e. I would like to rest

f. To play the guitar

g. Our favourite group

h. Rock music

Unit 19. My holiday plans: TRANSLATION/WRITING

1. Gapped translation

a. *I will go on holiday:* **Aniré de _______________**

b. *I will travel by car:* **Viatjaré en __________**

c. *We will spend one week there:*

________________ una setmana _________

d. *I will stay in a cheap hotel:*

______ quedaré a un hotel ____________

e. *We will eat and sleep every day:*

Menjarem i __________ cada _______

f. *If the weather is nice I will go to the beach:*

Si fa bon __________ aniré a la __________

g. *I will go shopping:* **Aniré a _____________**

2. Translate to English

a. Menjar

b. Comprar

c. Descansar

d. Fer turisme

e. Anar a la platja

f. Cada dia

g. En avió

h. Bussejar

i. Sortir al centre

3. Spot and correct the grammar and spelling mistakes

a. Faré desport

b. Pasaré una semana allà

c. quedaré a un hotel de luxe

d. Ens quedarnos a un hotel

e. M'agradaria jugar futbol

f. Sortirem al centro

g. Aniré la platja

h. Jugaré amb mes amics

4. Positive or negative? Write P or N

a. Serà divertit: **___P___**

b. Serà avorrit: _______

c. Serà agradable: _______

d. Serà relaxant: _______

e. Serà interessant: _______

f. Serà terrible: _______

g. Serà curiós: _______

h. Serà fastigós: _______

i. Serà fascinant: _______

j. Serà impressionant: _______

5. Translate into Catalan

a. I will rest

b. I will diving

c. We will go to the beach

d. I will sunbathe

e. I would like to go sightseeing

f. I will stay in…

g. …a cheap hotel

h. We will spend 2 weeks

i. I will go by plane

j. It will be fun

Revision Quickie 6: Daily Routine/House/Home life/Holidays

1. Match

Als afores	In the garden
Al bany	In the living room
A la cuina	In my bedroom
A casa meva	In my house
Al jardí	In the shower
A la meva habitació	In the dining room
Al menjador	In the bathroom
A la dutxa	In the kitchen
A la sala (d'estar)	On the outskirts

2. Complete with the missing letters

a. Em du______	*I shower*
b. M'__________	*I get up*
c. Mi_____ la tele	*I watch television*
d. Lle________ còmics	*I read comics*
e. Sur_____ de casa	*I leave home*
f. Arr_____ a l'escola	*I arrive at school*
g. Aga_____ el autobús	*I catch the bus*
h. Em ves_______	*I get dressed*
i Es________	*I have breakfast*

3. Spot and correct any of the sentences below which do not make sense

a. Em dutxo al sofà

b. Menjo a la dutxa

c. Preparo el menjar al llit

d. Em rento els cabells al menjador

e. Vaig a dormir a l'autobús

f. Jugo a ping-pong amb el meu gos

g. El sofà està al bany

h. Miro la tele al forn

i. Dormo a l'armari

j. Aparco el cotxe a l'habitació

4. Split sentences

Miro	l'autobús
Escolto	cereals
Llegeixo	la tele
Agafo	un cafè
Esmorzo	música
Aniré al Japó	còmics
Bec	deures
Pujo fotos	en avió
Faig els meus	a Instagram
Endreço	a cartes
Treballo a	la meva habitació
Jugo	l'ordinador

5. Match the opposites

Bo	Poc saludable
Simpàtic	Dolent
Fàcil	Bonic
Divertit	Antipàtic
Saludable	Difícil
Lleig	Avorrit
Car	Ràpid
Lent	Alt
Sovint	Barat
Mai	Poques vegades
Baix	Sempre

6. Complete with the missing words

a. Aniré al Japó _______ avió

b. Aniré a Itàlia _______ els meus pares

c. Mai jugo ____ futbol

d. Odio _______ criquet

e. Em quedo en un hotel ______ luxe

f. Vaig al parc una _________ a la setmana

g. Vaig ____ internet

h. Pujo fotos ____ Instagram

7. Draw a line in between each word

a. M'agradamoltjugarafutbol

b. Mirolateleiescoltomúsica

c. Almeutempslliurejugoavideojocs

d. AniréaAlemanyaencotxe

e. Emquedaréenunhoteldeluxe

f. Almatíaniréalaplatja

g. Sortirédefestaaquestdissabte

h. Maifaigelsdeures

8. Spot the translation mistakes and correct them

a. Vaig a dormir tard: *I go to sleep early*

b. Odio el bàsquet: *I hate volleyball*

c. Aniré a la piscina: *I am going to go to the beach*

d. No farem res: *I will not do anything*

e. Aniré a nedar: *I will og to run*

f. Viatjaré en cotxe: *I will travel by plane*

g. Em quedaré a un hotel car:

   I will stay in a cheap hotel

h. Miraré una pel·lícula: *I will watch a series*

9. Translate into English

a. Agafo l'avió

b. Aniré

c. Em quedaré

d. Em rento

e. Miro una pel·lícula

f. endreço la meva habitació

g. Sopo verdures

h. Esmorzo ous

i. No faig res

j. Treballo a l'ordinador

10. Translate into Catalan

a. I shower then I have breakfast

b. Tomorrow I am going to go to Japan

c. I tidy up my room every day

d. I never play basketball

e. I get up early

f. I eat a lot for breakfast

g. I will go to Italy by car

h. In my free time I play chess and read books

i. I spend many hours on the Internet

11. Translate into Catalan

a. I have dinner: S_ _ _

b. I watch: M_ _ _

c. I do: F_ _ _

d. I clean: N_ _ _ _ _ _

e. I read: Ll_ _ _ _ _ _

f. I work: T_ _ _ _ _ _ _

g. I rest: D_ _ _ _ _ _ _

h. I tidy up: E_ _ _ _ _ _

i. I catch: A_ _ _ _ _

Question Skills 4: Daily routine/House/Home life/Holidays

1. Complete the questions with the correct option

a. ___________________hora t'aixeques?

b. ___________________ passes el teu temps lliure?

c. ___________________fas després de l'escola?

d. ___________________hores passes a l'ordinador?

e. ___________________ jugues a la Play?

f. ___________________ no fas més esport?

g. ___________________ vas el divendres a la nit?

h. ___________________ és la teva habitació preferida?

On	A quina	Quantes	Què
Per què	Quina	Com	Amb qui

2. Split questions

A quina	no jugues a futbol amb nosaltres?
Què menges	vegades a la setmana vas al gimnàs?
Què	hora tornes a casa?
Amb	vas a córrer?
Per què	per esmorzar?
Quantes	qui jugues a escacs?
On	fas en el teu temps lliure?
Com passes	els teus pares a casa?
Ajudes	el teu temps lliure?

3. Match each statement below to one of the questions included in activity 1 above

a. Dues o tres

b. El passo jugant a l'ordinador

c. Amb el meu germà petit

d. Cap a les sis

e. Vaig a la discoteca amb el meu millor amic

f. Torno a casa

g. Perquè soc mandrós i no tinc temps

h. La meva (habitació), és clar

4. Translate into Catalan

a. Who?

b. When?

c. With whom?

d. Why?

e. How many? (feminine plural)

f. How much? (masculine singular)

g. Which ones?

h. Where to?

i. Do you do...?

j. Can you...?

k. Where is...?

l. How many hours?

m. How many people?

5. Translate

a. Where is your room?

b. Where do you go after school?

c. What do you do in your free time?

d. Until what time do you study?

e. How long do you spend on the Internet?

f. What is your favourite pastime?

g. What do you do to help in the house?

VOCABULARY TESTS

On the following pages you will find one vocabulary test for every unit in the book. You could set them as class assessments or as homeworks at the end of a unit. Students could also use them to practice independently.

1a. Translate the following sentences (worth one point each) into Catalan

What is your name?	
My name is Pau	
How old are you?	
I am five years old	
I am seven years old	
I am nine years old	
I am ten years old	
I am eleven years old	
I am twelve years old	
I am thirteen years old	
Score	/10

1b. Translate the following sentences (worth two points each) into Catalan

What is your brother called?	
What is your sister called?	
My brother is called Mario	
My sister is fourteen years old	
My brother is fifteen years old	
I don't have any siblings	
My name is Jean and I am French	
I have a brother who is called Felip	
I live in the capital of Japan	
I live in the capital of France	
Score	/20

1a. Translate the following sentences (worth one point each) into Catalan

My name is Sergio	
I am eleven years old	
I am fifteen years old	
I am eighteen years old	
The 3rd May	
The 4th April	
The 5th June	
The 6th September	
The 10th October	
The 8th July	
Score	**/10**

1b. Translate the following sentences (worth two points each) into Catalan

I am 17. My birthday is on 21st June	
My brother is called Julià. He is 19	
My sister is called Maria. She is 22	
My brother's birthday is on 23rd March	
My name is Rick. I am 15. My birthday is on 27th July	
My name is Gregori. I am 18. My birthday is on 30th June	
When is your birthday?	
Is your birthday in October or November?	
My brother is called Pere. His birthday is on 31st January	
Is your birthday in May or June?	
Score	**/20**

1a. Translate the following sentences (worth one point each) into Catalan

Black hair	
Dark brown (black) eyes	
Blond hair	
Blue eyes	
My name is Gabriela	
I am 12 years old	
I have long hair	
I have short hair	
I have green eyes	
I have brown eyes	
Score	/10

1b. Translate the following sentences (worth two points each) into Catalan

I have grey hair and grey eyes	
I have red straight hair	
I have curly white hair	
I have brown hair and brown eyes	
I wear glasses and have spikey hair	
I don't wear glasses and I have a beard	
My brother has blond hair and has a moustache	
My brother is 22 years old and has a crew cut	
Do you wear glasses?	
My sister has blue eyes and wavy black hair	
Score	/20

1a. Translate the following sentences (worth one point each) into Catalan

My name is	
I am from	
I live in	
In a house	
In a modern building	
In an old building	
On the outskirts	
In the centre	
On the coast	
In Zaragoza	
Score	**/10**

1b. Translate the following sentences (worth two points each) into Catalan

My brother is called Pau	
My sister is called Alexandra	
I live in an old building	
I live in a modern building	
I live in a beautiful house on the coast	
I live in an ugly house in the centre	
I am from Madrid but live in the centre of Buenos Aires	
I am 15 years old and I am Catalan	
I am Catalan, from Lleida but I live in Bogotá, in Colombia	
I live in a small apartment in the countryside	
Score	**/20**

1a. Translate the following sentences (worth one point each) into Catalan

My younger brother	
My older brother	
My older sister	
My younger sister	
My father	
My mother	
My uncle	
My auntie	
My male cousin	
My female cousin	
Score	**/10**

1b. Translate the following sentences (worth two points each) into Catalan

In my family there are four people	
My father, my mother and two brothers	
I don't get along with my older brother	
My older sister is 22	
My younger sister is 16	
My grandfather is 78	
My grandmother is 67	
My uncle is 54	
My auntie is 44	
My female cousin is 17	
Score	**/20**

1a. Translate the following sentences (worth one point each) into Catalan

Tall (masculine)	
Short (feminine)	
Ugly (masculine)	
Good-looking (masculine)	
Generous (masculine)	
Boring (feminine)	
Intelligent (masculine)	
Muscular (masculine)	
Good (feminine)	
Fat (masculine)	
Score	**/10**

1b. Translate the following sentences (worth two points each) into Catalan

My mother is strict and gentle	
My father is stubborn and friendly	
My older sister is intelligent and hard-working	
My younger sister is sporty	
In my family I have five people	
I get along with my older sister because she is nice	
I don't get along with my younger sister because she is annoying	
I love my grandparents because they are funny and generous	
What are your parents like?	
My uncle and auntie are fifty and I don't get along with them	
Score	**/20**

1a. Translate the following sentences (worth one point each) into Catalan

A horse	
A rabbit	
A dog	
A turtle	
A bird	
A parrot	
A duck	
A guinea pig	
A cat	
A mouse	
Score	/10

1b. Translate the following sentences (worth three points each) into Catalan

I have a white horse	
I have a green turtle	
At home we have two fish	
My sister has a spider	
I don't have pets	
My friend Pedro has a blue bird	
My cat is very fat	
I have a snake that is called Adam	
My duck is funny and noisy	
How many pets do you have at home?	
Score	/30

1a. Translate the following sentences (worth one point each) into Catalan

He is a cook	
He is a journalist	
She is a waitress	
She is a nurse	
He is a househusband	
She is a doctor	
He is a teacher	
She is a businesswoman	
He is a hairdresser	
She is a farmer	
Score	**/10**

1b. Translate the following sentences (worth three points each) into Catalan

My uncle is a cook	
My mother is a nurse	
My grandparents don't work	
My sister works as a teacher	
My auntie is an actress	
My (male) cousin is a student	
My (female) cousins are lawyers	
He doesn't like it because it is hard	
He likes it because it is gratifying	
He hates it because it is stressful	
Score	**/30**

1a. Translate the following sentences (worth two points each) into Catalan

He is taller than me	
He is more generous than her	
She is less tall than him	
He is slimmer than her	
She is better looking than him	
She is more talkative than me	
I am more funny than him	
My dog is less noisy	
My rabbit is more fun	
She is as talkative as me	
Score	**/20**

1b. Translate the following sentences (worth 3 points each) into Catalan

My brother is stronger than me	
My mother is tallerer than my father	
My uncle is better looking than my father	
My older sister is more talkative than my younger sister	
My sister and I are shorter than my cousins	
My grandfather is less strict than my grandmother	
My friend Paco is friendlier than my friend Felipe	
My rabbit is quieter than my duck	
My cat is fatter than my dog	
My mouse is faster than my turtle	
Score	**/30**

1a. Translate the following sentences (worth one point each) into Catalan

I have a pen	
I have a ruler	
I have a rubber	
In my bag	
In my pencil case	
My friend Arnau	
Pere has	
I don't have	
A purple exercise book	
A yellow pencil sharpener	
Score	**/10**

1b. Translate the following sentences (worth three points each) into Catalan

In my schoolbag I have four books	
I have a yellow pencil case	
I have a red schoolbag	
I don't have black markers	
There are two blue pens	
My friend Paco has a pencil sharpener	
Do you guys have a rubber?	
Do you have a red pen?	
Is there a ruler in your pencil case?	
What is there in your schoolbag?	
Score	**/30**

1a. Translate the following sentences (worth three points each) into Catalan

I don't like milk	
I love meat	
I don't like fish much	
I hate chicken	
Fruit is good	
Honey is healthy	
I prefer mineral water	
Milk is disgusting	
Chocolate is delicious	
Cheese is unhealthy	
Score	**/30**

1b. Translate the following sentences (worth five points each) into Catalan

I love chocolate because it is delicious	
I like apples a lot because they are healthy	
I don't like red meat because it is unhealthy	
I don't like sausages because they are unhealthy	
I love fish with potatoes	
I hate seafood because it is disgusting	
I like fruit because it is light and delicious	
I like spicy chicken with vegetables	
I like eggs because they are rich in protein	
Roast chicken is tastier than fried fish	
Score	**/50**

1a. Translate the following sentences (worth one point each) into Catalan

I have breakfast	
I have lunch	
I have afternoon 'snack'	
I have dinner	
It is delicious	
It is light	
It is disgusting	
It is refreshing	
It is healthy	
It is sweet	
Score	**/10**

1b. Translate the following sentences (worth three points each) into Catalan

I eat eggs and coffee for breakfast	
I have seafood for lunch	
I never have dinner	
For snack I have two 'toasts'	
In the morning I usually eat fruit	
I love meat because it is good	
From time to time I eat cheese	
In the evening I eat little	
We eat a lot of meat and fish	
I don't eat sweets often	
Score	**/30**

1a. Translate the following sentences (worth two points each) into Catalan

A red skirt	
A blue suit	
A green scarf	
Black trousers	
A white shirt	
A brown hat	
A yellow T-shirt	
Blue jeans	
A purple tie	
Grey shoes	
Score	**/20**

1b. Translate the following sentences (worth three points each) into Catalan

I often wear a black baseball cap	
At home I wear a blue track suit	
At school we wear a green uniform	
At the beach I wear a red bathing suit	
My sister always wears jeans	
My brother never wears a watch	
My mother wears branded clothes	
I very rarely wear suits	
My girlfriend wears a pretty jacket	
My brothers always wears trainers	
Score	**/30**

1a. Translate the following sentences (worth two points each) into Catalan

I do my homework	
I play football	
I go rock climbing	
I go cycling	
I do weights	
I go to the swimming pool	
I do sport	
I go horse riding	
I play tennis	
I go to the beach	
Score	**/20**

1b. Translate the following sentences (worth five points each) into Catalan

I never play basketball because it is boring	
I play PlayStation with my friends	
My father and I go fishing from time to time	
My brother and I go to the gym every day	
I do weights and go jogging every day	
When the weather is nice, we go hiking	
When the weather is bad, I play chess	
My father goes swimming at the weekend	
My younger brothers go to the park after school	
In my free time, I go rock climbing or to my friend's house	
Score	**/50**

THE LANGUAGE GYM

1a. Translate the following sentences (worth two points each) into Catalan

When the weather is nice	
When the weather is bad	
When it is sunny	
When it is cold	
When it is hot	
I go skiing	
I play with my friends	
I go to the mall	
I go to the gym	
I go on a bike ride	
Score	**/20**

1b. Translate the following sentences (worth four points each) into Catalan

When the weather is nice, I go jogging	
When it rains, we go to the sports centre and do weights	
At the weekend, I do my homework and a bit of sport	
When it is hot, she goes to the beach or goes cycling	
When I have time, I go jogging with my father	
When there are storms, we stay at home and play cards	
When it is sunny and the sky is clear, they go to the park	
On Fridays and Saturdays, I go clubbing with my girlfriend	
We never do sport. We play on the computer or on PlayStation	
When it snows, we go to the mountain and ski	
Score	**/40**

1a. Translate the following sentences (worth one point each) into Catalan

I get up	
I have breakfast	
I eat	
I drink	
I go to sleep	
Around six o' clock	
I rest	
At noon	
At midnight	
I do my homework	
Score	**/10**

1b. Translate the following sentences (worth three points each) into Catalan

Around 7.00 in the morning I have breakfast	
I shower then I get dressed	
I eat then I brush my teeth	
Around 8 o'clock in the evening I have dinner	
I go to school by bus	
I watch television in my room	
I go back home at 4.30	
From 6 to 7 I play on the computer	
Afterwards, around 11.30, I go to sleep	
My daily routine is simple	
Score	**/30**

THE LANGUAGE GYM

1a. Translate the following sentences (worth one point each) into Catalan

I live	
In a new house	
In an old house	
In a small house	
In a big house	
On the coast	
In the mountains	
In an ugly apartment	
On the outskirts	
In the centre of town	
Score	/10

1b. Translate the following sentences (worth three points each) into Catalan

In my house there are four rooms	
My favourite room is the kitchen	
I enjoy relaxing in the living room	
In my apartment there are seven rooms	
My parents live in a big house	
My uncle lives in a small house	
We live near the coast	
My friend Paco lives on a farm	
My cousins live in Barcelona	
My parents and I live in a cosy house	
Score	/30

1a. Translate the following sentences (worth one point each) into Catalan

I chat with my mother	
I play on the PlayStation	
I read magazines	
I read comics	
I watch films	
I listen to music	
I rest	
I do my homework	
I go on a bike ride	
I leave the house	
Score	**/10**

1b. Translate the following sentences (worth three points each) into Catalan

I never tidy up my room	
I rarely help my parents	
I brush my teeth three times a week	
I upload many photos into Instagram	
Every day I watch series on Netflix	
I have breakfast at around 7.30	
After school I rest in the garden	
When I have time, I play with my brother	
I usually leave home at 8 o'clock	
From time to time I watch a movie	
Score	**/30**

1a. Translate the following sentences (worth two points each) into Catalan

I will go	
I will stay	
I will play	
I will eat	
I will drink	
I will rest	
I will go sightseeing	
I will go to the beach	
I will do sport	
I will dance	
Score	**/20**

1b. Translate the following sentences (worth five points each) into Catalan

We will buy souvenirs and clothes	
I will stay in a cheap hotel near the beach	
We will stay there for three weeks	
I will spend two weeks there with my family	
We will go to Spain for two weeks and we will travel by plane	
I would like to go to Greece	
I would like to do sport, go to the beach and dance	
We will spend 3 weeks in Italy and we will stay in a camping	
We will stay in a luxury hotel near the beach	
We will go sightseeing and shopping every day	
Score	**/50**

The End

We hope you have enjoyed using this workbook and found it useful!

As many of you will appreciate, the penguin is a fantastic animal. At Language Gym, we hold it as a symbol of resilience, bravery and good humour; able to thrive in the harshest possible environments, and with, arguably the best gait in the animal kingdom (black panther or penguin, you choose). This is very applicable to the Catalan people, who are also brave, good-humoured and have a history of being resilient in very challenging circumstances. To find out more about the history of the Catalan language, ask your teacher ☺

There are several hidden penguins (pictures)in this book,
did you spot them all?